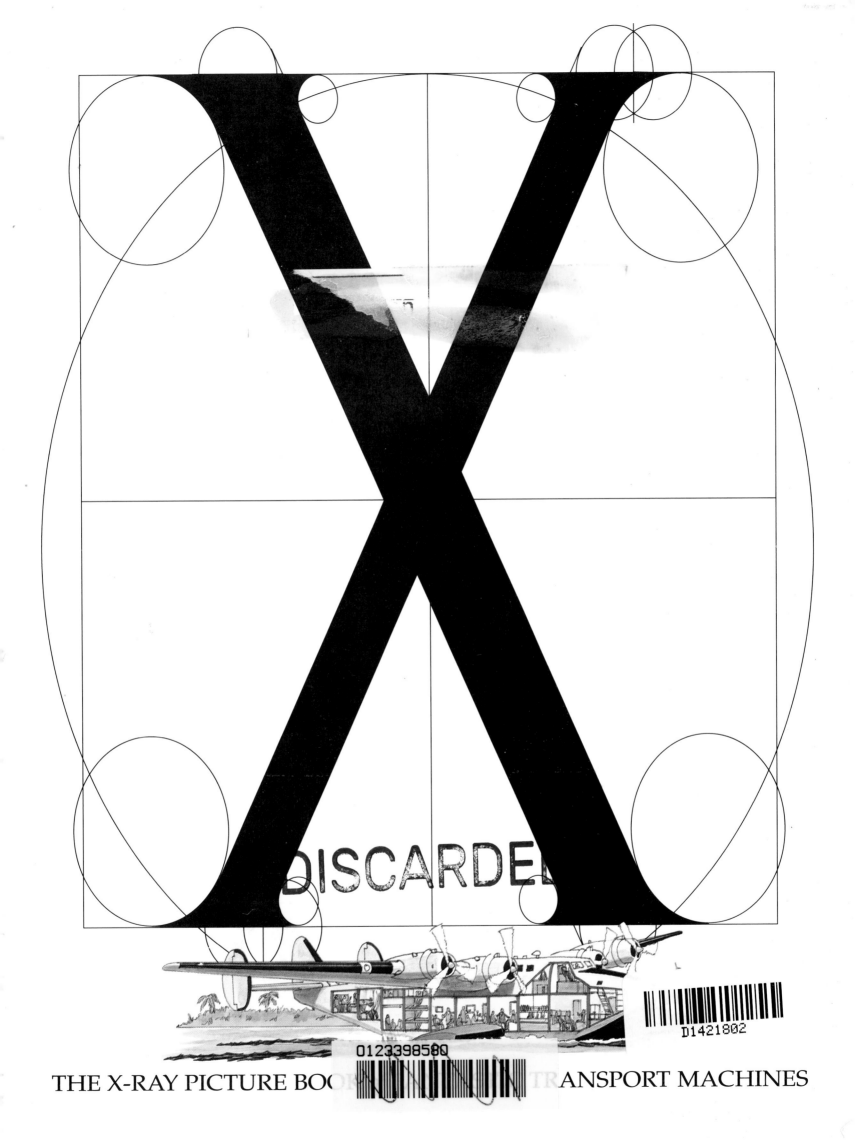

DISCARDED

THE X-RAY PICTURE BOOK OF TRANSPORT MACHINES

Author:
Chris Oxlade was educated in
Farnborough, Hampshire, and at the
University of Birmingham, where he
gained a degree in civil engineering.
He has written and edited a number
of books for children on computing,
science and technology. He lives in
Ilkley, West Yorkshire.

Consultant:
Andrew Nahum has written
extensively on transport subjects, and
his books include *The Rotary Aero
Engine* (HMSO, 1987) and *Alec
Issigonis* (Design Council, 1988). He
also acted as consultant on *Flight*,
a *Timelines* book.

Creator:
David Salariya was born in
Dundee, Scotland, where he studied
illustration and printmaking,
concentrating on book design in his
post-graduate year. He has illustrated
a wide range of books on botanical,
historical and mythical subjects. He
has designed and created the
Timelines, New View and *X-Ray Picture
Book* series for Watts Books. He lives
in Brighton with his wife, the
illustrator Shirley Willis.

David Salariya — *Series Editor*
Ruth Nason — *Senior Editor*
Jenny Millington — *Editor*
Andrew Nahum — *Consultant*

Artists:
Mark Bergin
Gordon C Davies
Nick Hewetson
John James
Gerald Wood

Artists
Mark Bergin p 14-15, p 22-23, p 24-25,
p 30-31, p 32-33; **Gordon C Davies** p 26-27,
p 28-29; **Nick Hewetson** p 6-7, p 8-9,
p 10-11, p 12-13, p 34-35, p 36-37, p 38-39,
p 40-41, p 42-43, p 44-45; **John James**
p 16-17, p 18-19; **Gerald Wood** p 20-21.

First Published in 1994
by Franklin Watts
This edition 2001

Franklin Watts
96 Leonard Street, London EC2A 4XD

Franklin Watts Australia
56 O'Riordan Street
Alexandria, Sydney, NSW 2015

ISBN 0 7496 4144 4

© The Salariya Book Co Ltd MCMXCIV

Printed in Belgium

A CIP catalogue record for this book is available
from the British Library.

The X-RAY PICTURE BOOK of FANTASTIC TRANSPORT MACHINES

Written by
CHRIS OXLADE

Created and designed by
DAVID SALARIYA

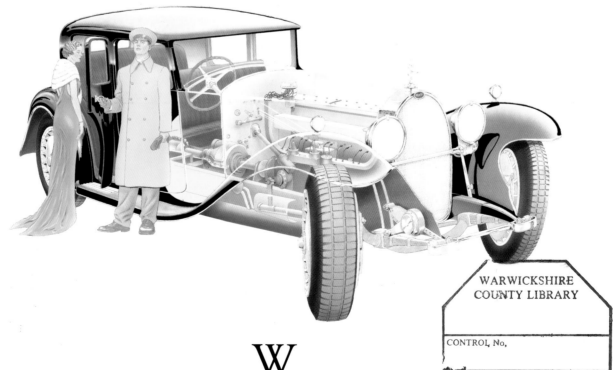

W
FRANKLIN WATTS
LONDON • SYDNEY

CONTENTS

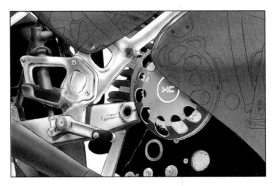
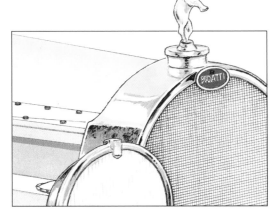

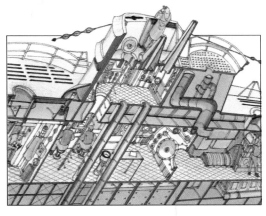

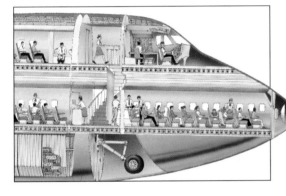

DUCATI 851 SUPERBIKE

THE DUCATI 851, with its stylish Italian looks and incredible acceleration and speed, is the machine of every biker's dreams. Ducati is one of the most famous names in motorbike manufacture, and the first 851 was built at their Bologna factory in 1987. Designer Massimo Bordi incorporated a number of new high-tech features, giving the bike the lightness and power necessary to challenge the likes of Yamaha and Honda on the race-track. It succeeded in 1990 and 1991, winning the World Superbike Championship twice in a row.

At the heart of the bike is an 851cc four-stroke engine. The two cylinders are at 90° to each other (an arrangement known as 90° V-twin), and each has four valves, two for fuel intake and two for exhaust gases. The engine also features fuel injection, where the fuel is introduced into the engine in accurately measured amounts using a pump (whereas

Underneath the sleek body of the 851 is a ladder-like frame constructed from steel tubing. The engine block itself forms one of the struts of the frame. All the other parts of the bike are bolted to this frame.

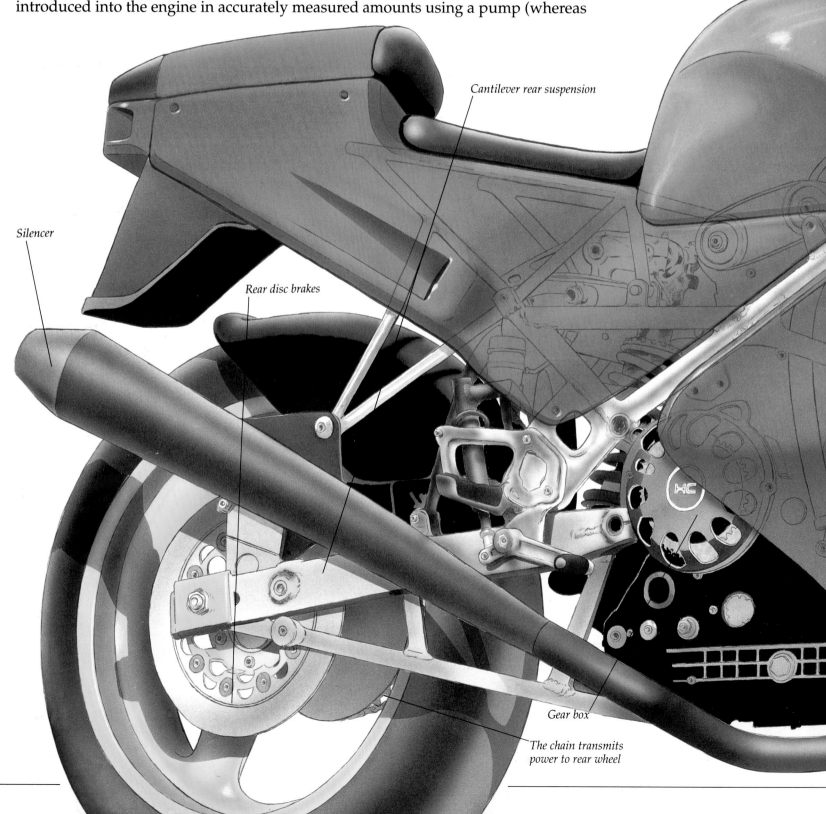

Cantilever rear suspension

Silencer

Rear disc brakes

Gear box

The chain transmits power to rear wheel

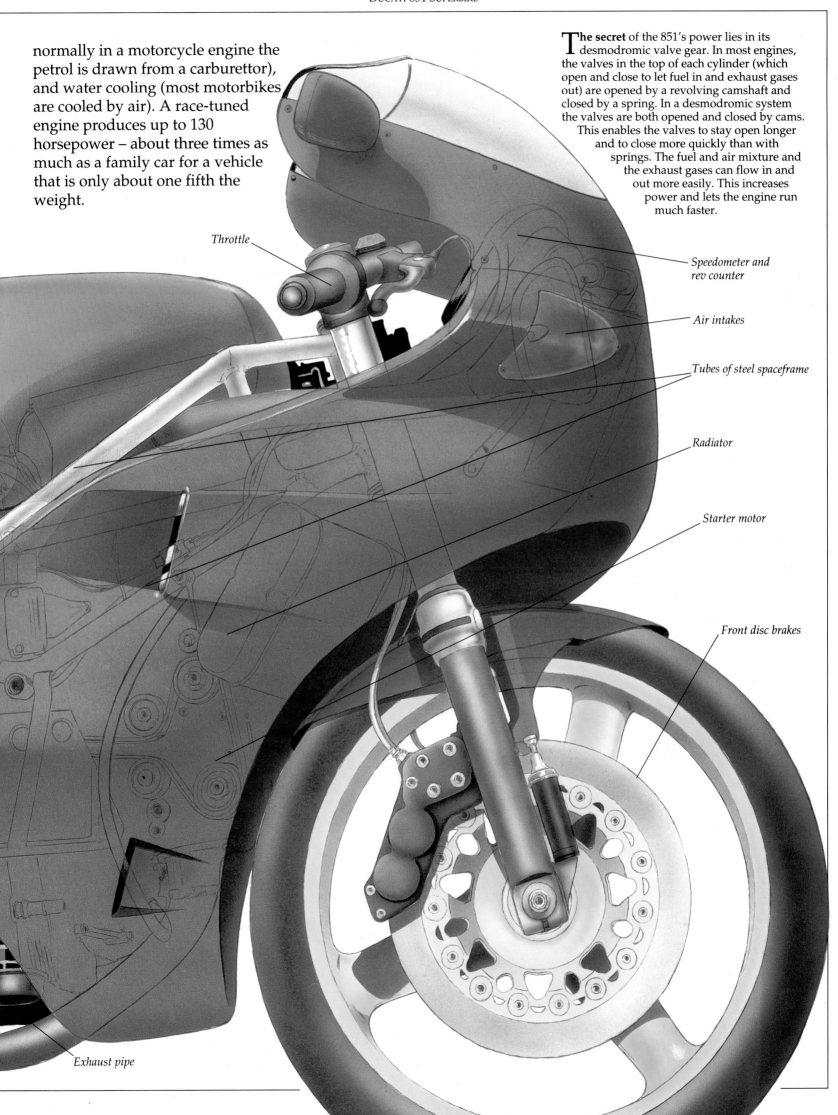

normally in a motorcycle engine the petrol is drawn from a carburettor), and water cooling (most motorbikes are cooled by air). A race-tuned engine produces up to 130 horsepower – about three times as much as a family car for a vehicle that is only about one fifth the weight.

The **secret** of the 851's power lies in its desmodromic valve gear. In most engines, the valves in the top of each cylinder (which open and close to let fuel in and exhaust gases out) are opened by a revolving camshaft and closed by a spring. In a desmodromic system the valves are both opened and closed by cams. This enables the valves to stay open longer and to close more quickly than with springs. The fuel and air mixture and the exhaust gases can flow in and out more easily. This increases power and lets the engine run much faster.

Throttle

Speedometer and rev counter

Air intakes

Tubes of steel spaceframe

Radiator

Starter motor

Front disc brakes

Exhaust pipe

Sitting astride an alcohol-heated boiler, the rider of the Michaux brothers' machine could zip along at a stately 15 km/h.

American engineer Lucius Copeland built a steam motorcycle from a penny farthing bicycle. It could achieve 20 km/h.

The rider used a small wheel to steer the three-wheeled von Saurbronne-Davis velocipede. The boiler was heated by petrol.

Daimler and Maybach's wooden-framed machine was a test-bed for the petrol engine that Daimler used in his first car.

William Henderson started motorcycle production in 1912 in Detroit. The first Henderson was a four-cylinder machine.

One of Britain's most famous motorcycle makers was Scott. Manufacture began in 1908.

Until Indian stopped manufacturing motorcycles in 1953, it was the leading maker in the United States. The most famous Indian creations were the Scout and the Chief.

The 1920s were the heyday of motorcycle manufacture. There were hundreds of companies, small and large, producing machines. Of the famous marque badges shown here, only BMW, which started life in 1932, still survives.

The rear wheels of early bikes had no suspension, which was the reason for the highly sprung saddle.

Drum brakes inside rear hub. There were no front brakes.

Harley Davidson is the oldest surviving motorcycle manufacturer in the world. The company's first model, the 9.35, became known as the "Silent Gray Fellow" because of its quiet running, the fact that it was only available in grey, and its reliability. Originally, power was transmitted to the rear wheel by a leather belt. There were no gears or clutch.

Chain drive

The magneto was like a dynamo (a machine that generates electricity). It was turned by the engine to produce electricity for the spark-plug.

Tool box

Silencer

Footrest

A 1914 Harley Davidson (above). The belt-drive of the early models was soon replaced with a chain-drive and a clutch, which temporarily disconnected the engine from the wheels and made stopping and starting much easier.

MOTORCYCLE History

The Belgian-built FN Four was manufactured from 1905. It was one of the first motorcycles with a four-cylinder engine. The cylinders were arranged in a line, a lay-out known as a straight-four.

THE EARLIEST MOTORCYCLES were simply pedal cycles with an engine bolted on. In 1868, French brothers Ernest and Pierre Michaux patented a machine consisting of an iron-wheeled bicycle with a small steam engine mounted under the saddle. Other steam-powered motorbikes followed, and although they seem rather impractical contraptions today, some went into production and were quite successful. The improvement of the internal combustion engine in 1876 by German engineer Nikolaus Otto revolutionised the transport world. The new engine's advantages over steam were greater power and less weight. In 1885, Gottlieb Daimler (later famous for his cars) and Wilhelm Maybach, both also German, built the first petrol-engined motorcycle. Designers tried various positions for the engine, such as behind the rear wheel and even on a separate trolley, but the "classic" arrangement where the engine is mounted centrally between the wheels eventually became standard. This layout was designed by Frenchmen Michael and Eugene Werner, whose 1901 machine also had handlebar twist grips for engine control. Motorcycle design then advanced rapidly. Many new manufacturers opened factories in Europe and America, and the sport of motorcycle racing began. By the beginning of World War One in 1914, motorcycles had actually begun to look like motorcycles, rather than bicycles with motors.

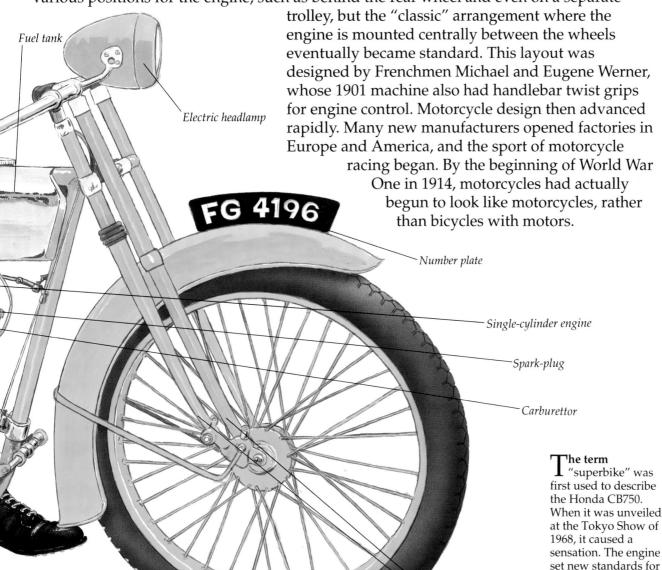

Fuel tank

Electric headlamp

FG 4196

Number plate

Single-cylinder engine

Spark-plug

Carburettor

Front forks

Pedals (hidden behind the rider's leg in this picture) were used for starting and in case of breakdown.

BMW launched their first-ever motorcycle, the twin-cylinder R32, in Paris in 1932.

A pressed steel frame (rather than tubes) made the German Zundapp K800 unique in 1932.

Ariel continued to build their Square Four machine in Britain for 27 years after it first appeared in 1931.

One of the fastest production motorcycles of the 1950s, the British Vincent Black Shadow.

The late 1960s saw the Japanese enter the world motorcycle market. This is the 1968 Honda CB750.

The term "superbike" was first used to describe the Honda CB750. When it was unveiled at the Tokyo Show of 1968, it caused a sensation. The engine set new standards for power, smoothness and reliability for a production motorcycle. Other manufacturers followed Honda – and the superbike era had begun.

Kawasaki motorcycles are renowned for their speed. Streamlined design helped make the Kawasaki ZX-10 the fastest road-going motorcycle of 1988. It reached 268 km/h on a test track.

BUGATTI ROYALE

Ettore Bugatti's clever styling meant the huge Royale did not look cumbersome.

The cast-iron block of the 8-cylinder engine was 1.4m long and the complete engine weighed 349 kg.

The wheelbase was 4.3m. Two strong chassis members ran the length of the car for support.

The gearbox of the Royale was located in the rear axle. The flexibility and power of the huge engine required only 3 gears to run efficiently and smoothly.

Running-board

Chauffeur in uniform

Drive shaft to rear-wheel drive

Flywheel and clutch

Steering column

Steel chassis sections

After its test period, the prototype Royale was used by the Bugatti family. The body was changed several times; this was the saloon version.

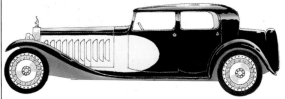

IN THE 1920s, STYLE WAS ALL-IMPORTANT. The rich and famous wore beautiful clothes and travelled to their high-society functions in great comfort. Of all the symbols of wealth and status, there was none greater than the ownership of a Bugatti Royale Type 41. The Royale was designed in Italy by Ettore Bugatti in the early 1920s to be the car of kings and queens. It was huge (6.7 metres long overall) but not lumbering. Under the bonnet (almost large enough to park a small car on) was a huge 12.7-litre, eight-cylinder engine.

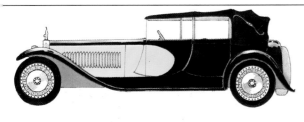

When production started, the Bugatti Royale was made available with a choice of several different body styles.

The Bugatti Royale was not a mass-produced car. Apart from the prototype, only six were ever built, and of those, only three were sold – at three times as much as a Rolls-Royce would have cost. As with all luxury cars of the day, when the customer ordered, he or she would discuss the coachwork design with the manufacturer, who then commissioned the body from a separate coachbuilder. In the case of the Royale, no two bodies were the same, but each one was a creation of sumptuous luxury. The Bugatti Royale was not a commercial success for the company, but it made the Bugatti name even more famous. Today, because of its rarity, a Bugatti Royale is worth a fortune – in 1987, a 1931 Royale with bodywork by the coachbuilder Kellner was sold at auction for £5.5 million.

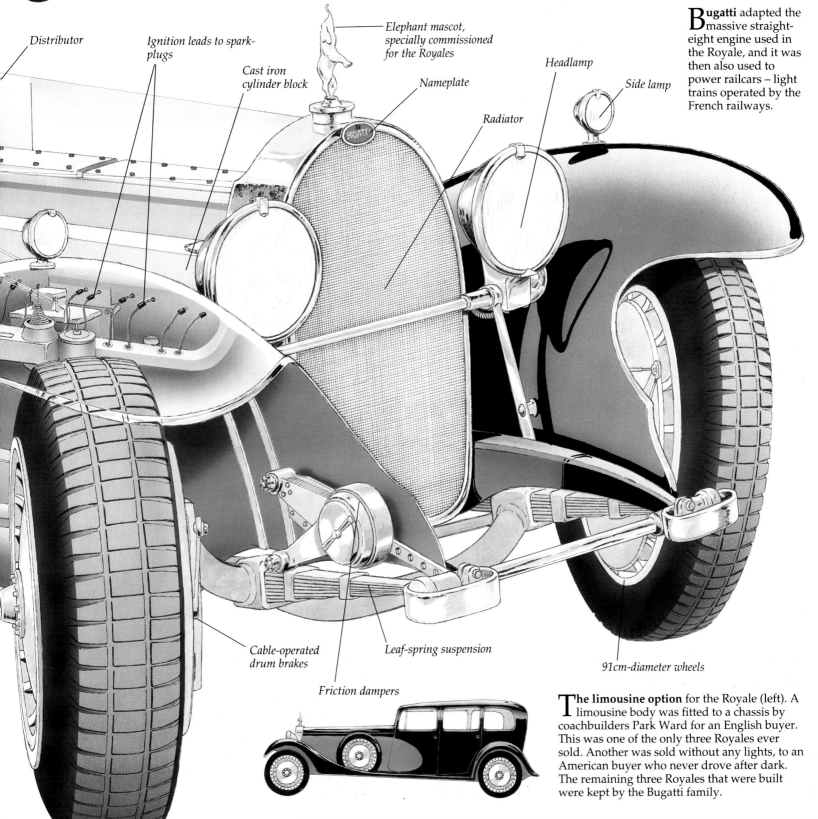

Distributor

Ignition leads to spark-plugs

Cast iron cylinder block

Elephant mascot, specially commissioned for the Royales

Nameplate

Headlamp

Side lamp

Radiator

Bugatti adapted the massive straight-eight engine used in the Royale, and it was then also used to power railcars – light trains operated by the French railways.

Cable-operated drum brakes

Leaf-spring suspension

Friction dampers

91cm-diameter wheels

The limousine option for the Royale (left). A limousine body was fitted to a chassis by coachbuilders Park Ward for an English buyer. This was one of the only three Royales ever sold. Another was sold without any lights, to an American buyer who never drove after dark. The remaining three Royales that were built were kept by the Bugatti family.

THE LEGENDARY Bugatti

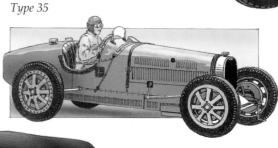

Type 13

ETTORE BUGATTI was born in Milan, Italy, on 15 September 1881. He originally studied art, but took a job as a test driver and mechanic at a Milanese motorcycle manufacturer, and while there he designed and built his first car, using both his artistic and his engineering skills. In 1909, while working as technical manager for Deutz in Cologne, Germany, Bugatti designed and built a small, light car, which he called the *Pur Sang*. That car was the basis of the Type 13, the first car to bear the now-famous Bugatti name. Production began with borrowed money in 1910, at Bugatti's new factory (an old dyeing works) at Molsheim, near Strasbourg. The workforce grew and by 1911, seventy-five Type 13 Bugattis had been built.

The Bugatti emblem first appeared on a car in 1910. By the 1930s, owning a Bugatti was the height of fashion. Bugatti was never a big company, but it was among the best.

The 1327cc Type 13 was the first Bugatti car to go into production. About 500 were built at the Molsheim factory. It was one of the first small cars to feature a 4-cylinder engine, which until then had been limited to use in large touring cars. This made the Type 13 smoother to drive than its competitors, whose engines still had one or two large cylinders.

The first production Bugatti powered by an engine featuring 8 cylinders rather than 4 was the Type 30, first built in 1922. The cylinders were all in a row, an arrangement known as a "straight-eight".

Type 22

One of Bugatti's early racing models, the Type 22. This was built in 1913-14, and was probably very uncomfortable to drive.

The early Bugattis were small, light cars with a good turn of speed. The various Types were manufactured in road-going production versions and also in racing trim. The 1920s and 1930s were the heyday of motor racing, and Bugatti's success on the track, mainly with the Type 35, boosted sales of the production cars. The period from 1924 to 1927 saw Bugatti cars win 1,851 races. In the 1930s Bugatti began to build larger luxury cars, but the racing side continued, with cars based on the production models.

Type 30

Every Bugatti model featured the famous radiator, shaped like an inverted horseshoe.

Type 35

The Type 35 had cast aluminium wheels, which were not as strong as wire ones.

Type 40 tourer

Bugatti chose the French Grand Prix of 1924 to launch the Type 35 (above). To improve the car's power, a supercharger, like those used by Bugatti's racing rivals, was later added.

The Type 40 tourer (left) could carry four people in comfort. It was manufactured from 1925 onwards with a 1.4-litre straight-four engine. In the later Type 40A, engine capacity was increased to 1.6 litres.

Type 49 saloon

The Bugatti company's early fame stemmed from the success of its cars on the race-track. The first win was by a Type 13, driven by Ettore Bugatti's friend and mechanic, Friderich, in the Grand Prix of Le Mans in 1911. Many more victories followed, the price of Bugatti cars increased, and every car that rolled off the production line sold straight away. During World War One, Bugatti worked on designs for a series of aero-engines, but they proved to be unreliable, and did not enter production. Success returned after the war with more Grand Prix wins, including a sensational first four places in one race in 1921. The Type 35 (see opposite page), designed in 1923-24, was probably the most famous Bugatti of all, and the most beautiful Grand Prix car of the late 1920s and 1930s.

Ettore Bugatti's eldest son, Jean, was also a great stylist. He designed many classic Bugattis of the 1930s and was responsible for the company's racing programme. Jean Bugatti died in 1939 while testing a Type 59 sports racing car. Ettore Bugatti died in 1947, and in reality the company died with him.

Between 1930 and 1934, Bugatti produced the Type 49 (above). Like all the larger Bugattis, it was available in various styles, such as the saloon version shown here. The Type 49 was one of the deluxe cars built to sell to rich and famous people once the Bugatti name had been established by the racing cars.

Under the bonnet of this 1934 GP Bugatti (below) Type 49 was an 8-cylinder, 3257cc engine. This "straight-eight" had two spark-plugs on each cylinder, giving more efficient ignition of the fuel and air mixture in the cylinders.

Jean Bugatti was responsible for the body design of a number of the later Bugattis, including the Type 57 (below). This car first appeared in the mid-1930s and was one of the last models. Several versions were available to the customer, including the sports tourer. The Type 57 was the basis for the first and only post-war Bugatti, the Type 101.

The evolution of the Type 57 was not smooth. Ettore Bugatti did not allow some of Jean's ideas, such as independent front suspension, to be included. The rear axle had to be redesigned, and the engine capacity was increased.

The Type 57 (below) was the most impressive touring sports car of the 1930s. The "tank-bodied" version of this car, which had a wide, streamlined body shell, won Le Mans in 1936 and 1939.

Type 57 sports tourer

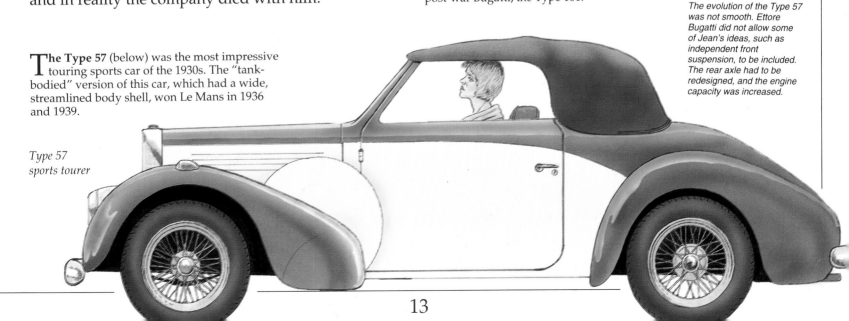

THE ORIENT EXPRESS

Georges Nagelmackers, founder of the Orient Express. His Wagons-Lits carriages ran on several routes, such as Paris–Vienna (from 1873), before he negotiated the route to Istanbul.

THE ORIENT EXPRESS was the world's most fabulous train. In its heyday, between the 1880s and the 1930s, it was the most luxurious way for the rich and famous to travel across Europe. It had two main attractions. First was the magic and mystery of the final name on the departure board – Istanbul, the gateway to the Orient. Second was the no-expense-spared luxury of the accommodation and food. The first Orient Express left Gare de l'Est in Paris on 4 October 1883.

The coat of arms of the Compagnie Internationale des Wagons-Lits et des Grands Express Européens. The company was originally just the Compagnie Internationale des Wagons-Lits – the Grand European Express part was added in 1883. The coat of arms and the name appeared on every carriage.

The carriages shown here are of the later type, built in the 1920s.

Leather seating

Dining-car

Flexible "corridor" linking two cars

Luggage labels were attached to every bag that was carried. Each passenger was allowed to take 150kg of baggage on the train.

The idea for the Orient Express came from the US. Belgian engineer Georges Nagelmackers was impressed by the comfortable Pullman cars he saw there, and the fact that their inventor George Pullman had negotiated with local rail companies for the carriages to be passed from one company to the next, without the need for the passengers to change trains. Nagelmackers decided to try the idea in Europe. He began building luxury sleeping carriages, and founded the Compagnie Internationale des Wagons-Lits. The sleeping-car compartments were miniature sitting-rooms which could be converted into bedrooms at night. Inside were comfortable armchairs, expensive carpets and silk coverings on the walls. In the dining-car, decorated with gold-framed etchings, passengers ate lavish five-course meals.

The staff and uniforms of the Orient Express. In overall charge was the Chef du Brigade, responsible for the sleeping-car conductors and the dining-car staff. The Chef du Brigade also personally took care of royal passengers.

The dining-car was run like a top restaurant. In charge was the Maître d'Hôtel, and under him worked the head waiter and waiters. Soot from the engine made white uniforms impractical, so Orient Express waiters wore blue.

The most coveted job was that of a sleeping-car conductor. Each conductor was responsible for all the needs of the passengers in his sleeping car, a job requiring command of several languages and a lot of discretion.

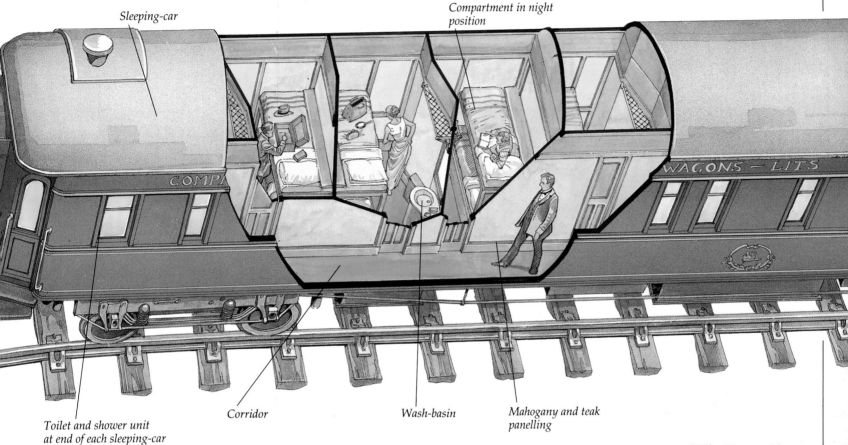

Sleeping-car

Compartment in night position

Toilet and shower unit at end of each sleeping-car

Corridor

Wash-basin

Mahogany and teak panelling

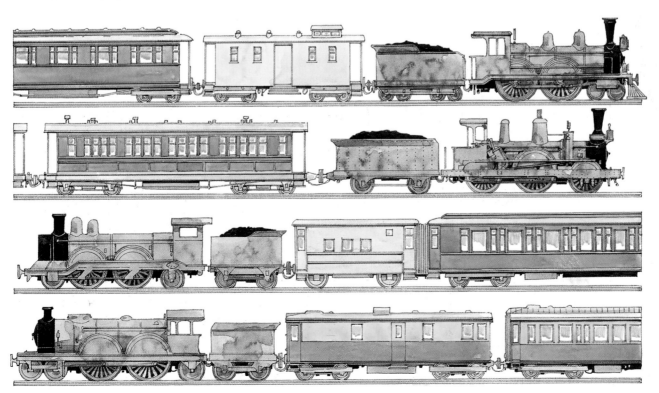

The Wagons-Lits carriages (left) that made up the Orient Express changed over the years. The Wagons-Lits company did not own its own locomotives – there were frequent changes as the train moved into areas controlled by different railway companies. From top to bottom are: the engine that made the first Wagons-Lits company journey in 1872; a simple two-cylinder engine pulling the Orient Express in 1883; a train of 1898 as it appeared on an advertising poster; and a steam locomotive hauling restored carriages of the Nostalgic Orient Express in 1977.

TRAVELLING FROM
Paris to Istanbul

In the 1920s and 1930s, the romance and intrigue of the Orient Express were so great that the train became the setting for several novels and films. Among them were Graham Greene's Stamboul Train *(1932), Agatha Christie's* Murder on the Orient Express *(1934) and Alfred Hitchcock's* The Lady Vanishes *(1938). James Bond also travelled on the train in the film* From Russia with Love *(1963).*

King Boris III of Bulgaria (who reigned 1918-43) was train mad, and often stood on the footplate of the locomotive of the Orient Express as it passed through his country.

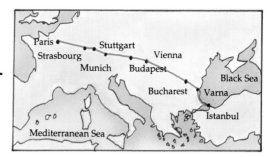

This map (left) shows the route of the original Orient Express. Passengers made the last part of the journey to Istanbul by steamer on the Black Sea.

Passenger cars

Fuel tender

Driver's cab

Track gauge (the distance between the rails) in Spain and Portugal differed from the rest of Europe. Nagelmackers had separate carriages built for the Spanish market.

Rear bogie wheels (2)

SERVICES ON THE ORIGINAL ROUTE of the Orient Express, north of the Alps, were disrupted by World War One. After the war, in 1919, a new route was opened. Leaving Gare de Lyon in Paris, the train went further south, into Italy through the newly-opened Simplon Tunnel, and through Yugoslavia to Istanbul. This service was known as the Simplon-Orient Express, and was the best-known route. In the 1930s there were four "Orient" routes: the original Orient Express, the Simplon-Orient Express, the Ostend-Vienna-Orient Express (Ostend to Bucharest) and the Arlberg-Orient Express (Paris to Bucharest). These were not separate trains that each travelled the length of one route. Carriages were combined at some stations and divided up at others, and the locomotives were changed as the trains used tracks owned by different railway companies. It was a complex feat of organisation by the company, but was largely unnoticed by the passengers. The Orient Express service was suspended during World War Two and never really recovered. The standard of service was not the same, and Wagons-Lits carriages formed only some of the rolling stock. The last real Orient Express left Paris on 20 May 1961. In 1982, a Venice Simplon-Orient Express (which runs from London to Venice) was started using restored Wagons-Lits carriages.

Scenes of Istanbul on a poster advertising the Orient Express. Train times are also listed.

Buying a ticket for a journey on the Orient Express. Travelling in the Wagons-Lits carriages is very expensive.

A porter transports the baggage to the sleeping-car. Passengers are allowed to take huge amounts of luggage onto the train.

The passengers are shown into their own sleeping-car compartment by the conductor, who will look after them.

The passengers settle down in their compartment. The train leaves Paris at 7.30 p.m. so that the first meal served on board is dinner.

In his small compartment at the end of the sleeping-car carriage, the sleeping-car conductor presses a gentleman's trousers.

Soon after leaving Paris, the passengers make their way to the dining car, where they choose from the dishes on the extensive menu.

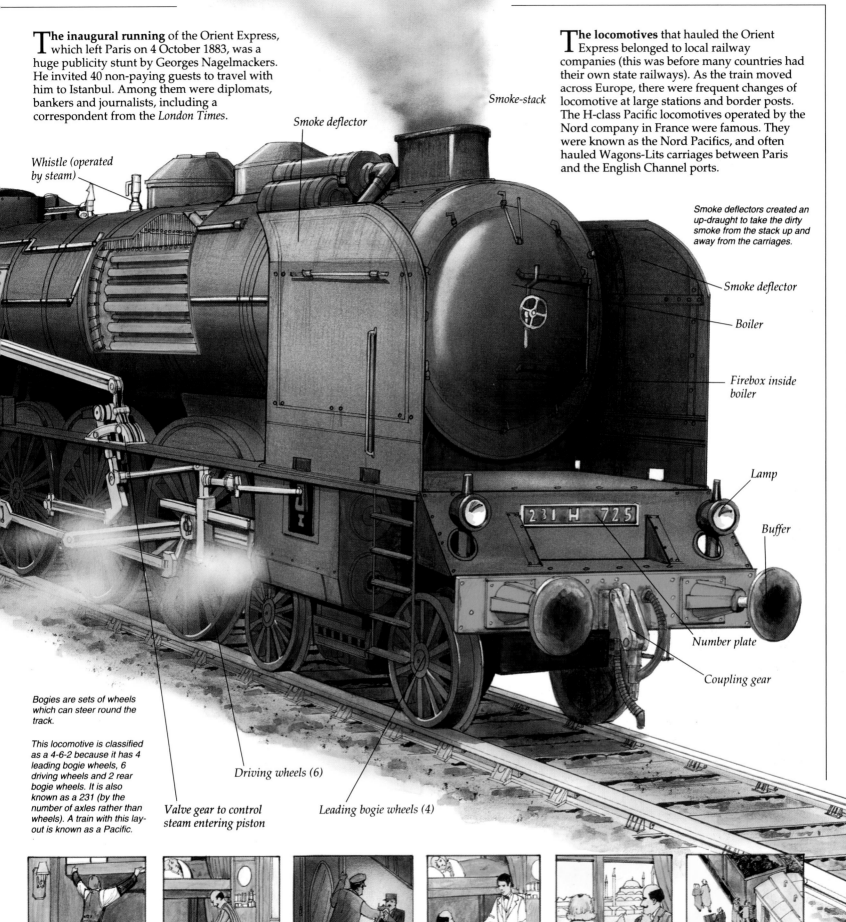

The inaugural running of the Orient Express, which left Paris on 4 October 1883, was a huge publicity stunt by Georges Nagelmackers. He invited 40 non-paying guests to travel with him to Istanbul. Among them were diplomats, bankers and journalists, including a correspondent from the *London Times*.

The locomotives that hauled the Orient Express belonged to local railway companies (this was before many countries had their own state railways). As the train moved across Europe, there were frequent changes of locomotive at large stations and border posts. The H-class Pacific locomotives operated by the Nord company in France were famous. They were known as the Nord Pacifics, and often hauled Wagons-Lits carriages between Paris and the English Channel ports.

Smoke-stack

Smoke deflector

Whistle (operated by steam)

Smoke deflectors created an up-draught to take the dirty smoke from the stack up and away from the carriages.

Smoke deflector

Boiler

Firebox inside boiler

Lamp

231 H 725

Buffer

Bogies are sets of wheels which can steer round the track.

This locomotive is classified as a 4-6-2 because it has 4 leading bogie wheels, 6 driving wheels and 2 rear bogie wheels. It is also known as a 231 (by the number of axles rather than wheels). A train with this lay-out is known as a Pacific.

Number plate

Coupling gear

Driving wheels (6)

Valve gear to control steam entering piston

Leading bogie wheels (4)

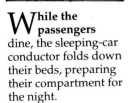

While the passengers dine, the sleeping-car conductor folds down their beds, preparing their compartment for the night.

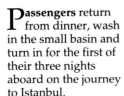

Passengers return from dinner, wash in the small basin and turn in for the first of their three nights aboard on the journey to Istanbul.

As the passengers sleep, the train rolls smoothly through the night. At border crossings, the conductors show passports and papers.

In the morning, the passengers are woken by the conductor. During breakfast their compartment is tidied for day use.

After two and a half days of travelling, the minarets of the hundreds of mosques in Istanbul come into view.

Journey's end in Istanbul, the gateway to the Orient. Some passengers will continue their journeys into Asia by other means.

The size of the *Queen Mary* (above) in relation to some famous buildings.

THE QUEEN MARY

THE *QUEEN MARY* was one of the largest and most luxurious ocean liners ever built. A voyage as a first-class passenger was one of the great travel experiences, and was enjoyed by numerous rich, famous and royal people. The *Queen Mary* was launched in September 1934, and made its maiden voyage on 27 May 1936. The liner crossed and recrossed the Atlantic, always passing the slightly bigger *Queen Elizabeth*, in mid-ocean. The *Queen Mary* carried nearly 2000 passengers in three classes – first or cabin class, second or tourist class, and third class. Feeding and entertaining the passengers, and keeping the ship's machinery running involved over 1000 officers and crew. The *Queen Mary* could cross the Atlantic in four days at a speed of over 30 knots (55 km/h).

Cargo hold hatchway

Each of the four anchors weighed 16 tonnes and was on a chain 330 fathoms (600 metres) long.

Main mast

Wheelhouse

Flying bridge

The *Queen Mary* was a huge ship. It was 311 metres long and 36 metres wide in the beam (at the middle). From the promenade deck, it was a 20-metre vertical drop into the sea, and the hull continued for another 12 metres under the water. The *Queen Mary* weighed over 81,000 tonnes.

Sun deck

Double-bottomed hull

Pilot's launch

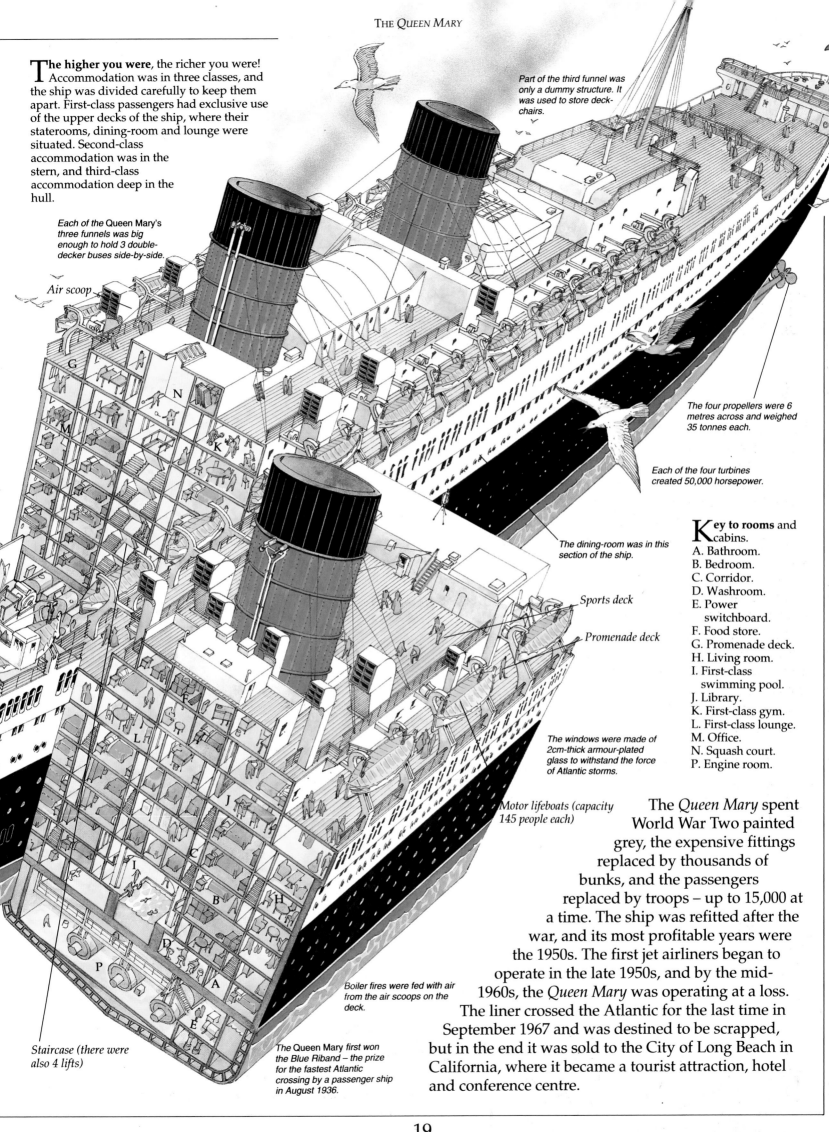

The higher you were, the richer you were! Accommodation was in three classes, and the ship was divided carefully to keep them apart. First-class passengers had exclusive use of the upper decks of the ship, where their staterooms, dining-room and lounge were situated. Second-class accommodation was in the stern, and third-class accommodation deep in the hull.

Each of the Queen Mary's three funnels was big enough to hold 3 double-decker buses side-by-side.

Air scoop

Part of the third funnel was only a dummy structure. It was used to store deck-chairs.

The four propellers were 6 metres across and weighed 35 tonnes each.

Each of the four turbines created 50,000 horsepower.

The dining-room was in this section of the ship.

Key to rooms and cabins.
A. Bathroom.
B. Bedroom.
C. Corridor.
D. Washroom.
E. Power switchboard.
F. Food store.
G. Promenade deck.
H. Living room.
I. First-class swimming pool.
J. Library.
K. First-class gym.
L. First-class lounge.
M. Office.
N. Squash court.
P. Engine room.

Sports deck

Promenade deck

The windows were made of 2cm-thick armour-plated glass to withstand the force of Atlantic storms.

Motor lifeboats (capacity 145 people each)

Boiler fires were fed with air from the air scoops on the deck.

Staircase (there were also 4 lifts)

The Queen Mary first won the Blue Riband – the prize for the fastest Atlantic crossing by a passenger ship in August 1936.

The Queen Mary spent World War Two painted grey, the expensive fittings replaced by thousands of bunks, and the passengers replaced by troops – up to 15,000 at a time. The ship was refitted after the war, and its most profitable years were the 1950s. The first jet airliners began to operate in the late 1950s, and by the mid-1960s, the Queen Mary was operating at a loss. The liner crossed the Atlantic for the last time in September 1967 and was destined to be scrapped, but in the end it was sold to the City of Long Beach in California, where it became a tourist attraction, hotel and conference centre.

BUILDING THE
Queen Mary

THERE WAS GREAT RIVALRY between the various shipping companies that operated the transatlantic liners. Cunard planned the *Queen Mary* and the *Queen Elizabeth* to run a weekly service between Southampton and New York, and they were to be the biggest ships ever built. The *Queen Mary* was ordered in 1930, but this was the time of the "Great Depression", and work soon stopped for lack of money. The ship was saved by the merger of Cunard and White Star, previously a rival line, and the injection of government money. Work restarted in 1932. The hull was constructed of steel girders and covered in 2.5cm-thick steel plating. Over 10,000,000 rivets were used. Until launch day, the *Queen Mary* was known as Job 534 – the number allotted by John Brown's, the Scottish shipyard where the liner was built.

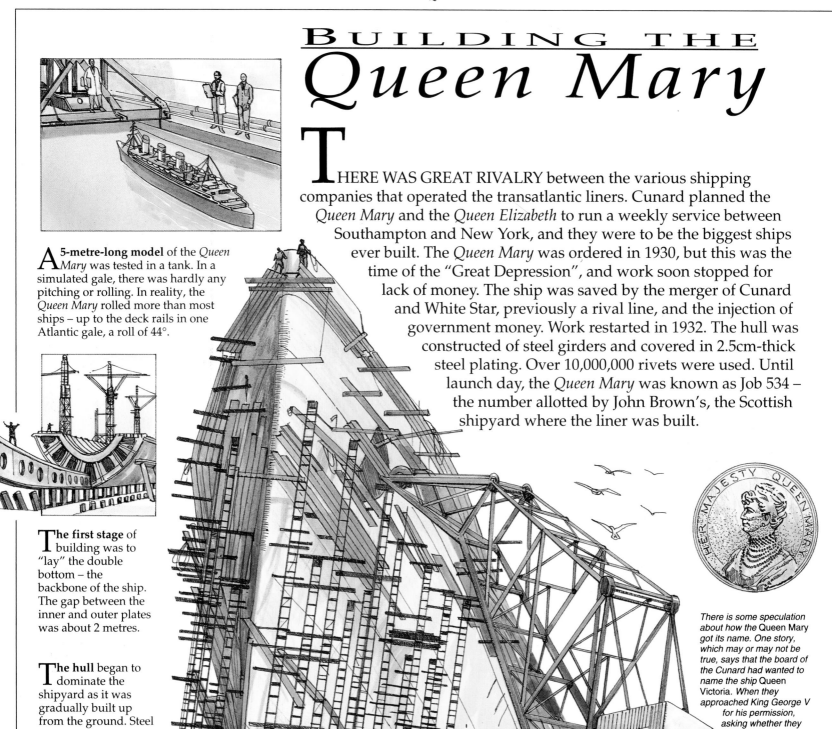

A **5-metre-long model** of the *Queen Mary* was tested in a tank. In a simulated gale, there was hardly any pitching or rolling. In reality, the *Queen Mary* rolled more than most ships – up to the deck rails in one Atlantic gale, a roll of 44°.

The **first stage** of building was to "lay" the double bottom – the backbone of the ship. The gap between the inner and outer plates was about 2 metres.

The **hull** began to dominate the shipyard as it was gradually built up from the ground. Steel plates were riveted to the framework, and decks and partitions were added inside the hull.

There is some speculation about how the Queen Mary *got its name. One story, which may or may not be true, says that the board of the Cunard had wanted to name the ship* Queen Victoria. *When they approached King George V for his permission, asking whether they could name their new ship "after the greatest woman who had ever been queen of England", he replied that he was sure his wife –* Queen Mary *– would be delighted!*

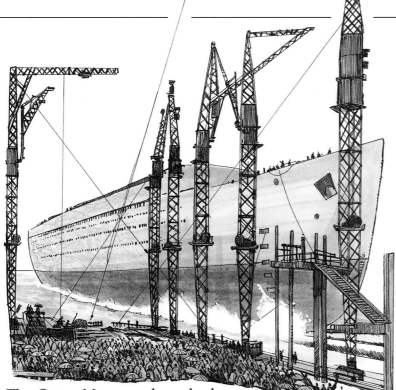

The *Queen Mary* was launched
as an empty shell, which was towed to the fitting-out
basin where work began to add the mechanical
fittings, such as engines, pumps and fuel tanks, and
the décor in the cabins and day-rooms. Every day for
over a year, an army of welders, plumbers, electricians,
painters, panellers and polishers went aboard to
transform the shell into a ship. Then came the *Queen
Mary*'s performance trials at sea. The river authority
had taken eighteen months to dredge a channel in the
river Clyde deep enough for the ship to move out to
sea – and the hull still scraped the bottom. For the
maiden voyage, and for every voyage after that, a
huge quantity of supplies was needed. The shopping
list for feeding over 2000 passengers with the best food
and wine for just five days included 20,000 kilos of
vegetables and 40,000 bottles of beer.

The largest and most magnificent of the
rooms on the *Queen Mary* was the cabin-
class dining-room (right). Situated in the centre
of the ship, it was three decks high in the
middle, 48 metres long and 36 metres wide (the
entire width of the ship). The panelling was in
browns, gold and bronze, and the upholstered
seating was in rose pink. At one sitting, 815
passengers could be fed. The menu had at least
a dozen courses on offer.

The *Queen Mary* was launched on 26
September 1934. Thousands of people
crowded the shipyard to watch the King and
Queen perform the ceremony. In the morning,
the weight of the ship had been transferred onto
the sliding cradles that would carry it down the
slipway to the water. The slipway had been
covered with 200 tonnes of tallow and soap,
and 2000 tonnes of chain had been attached to
the hull to stop it sliding too far. As the Queen
pressed the launching button, Job 534, now the
Queen Mary, gradually gathered speed, and a
minute later was afloat.

Cabin-class
staterooms
(above) were
luxurious, with
private bathrooms
and a telephone.

Every tourist-class
cabin (below) had
a wash-basin, and
most had a private
toilet.

In the cabin-class
restaurant was a
decorative map (left)
of the Atlantic.
Passengers could keep
track of their voyage
by watching a crystal
model of the *Queen
Mary*, lit with a bulb,
move across the map.

On the lower
decks under the
bridge was the cabin-
class swimming pool
(below). It had deep
and shallow ends and
heated water. There
was also a tourist-
class pool further back
in the ship, but no
third-class pool. The
pools had to be
emptied in rough
weather.

A typical day for a
cabin-class
passenger on the
Queen Mary.

A morning could be
passed reading a
book from the library
or browsing in the
shopping mall.

Midday. Choosing
from the
luncheon menu was
probably the most
taxing task.

There was a choice
of deck games and
sports, or you could
go to a squash court
or the gymnasium.

Early evening
could be spent
relaxing in the
cocktail bar and
observation lounge.

After dinner and
before bed, there
was dancing in the
cabin-class lounge or
the verandah grill.

U-BOAT VII-C

THE *UNTERSEEBOOTE* or U-boat was one of the most deadly weapons of the Second World War. Six hundred and fifty Type VII U-boats were launched by the German navy during the war, and they were often able to approach enemy shipping without being detected. Each U-boat carried fourteen torpedoes which blew holes in enemy ships and sank them. Travelling on the surface, powered by its diesel engines, the U-boat could manage 17 knots (31 km/h). Underwater, with propulsion provided by electric motors, speed decreased to 7.5 knots (13 km/h).

Living and working as part of a U-boat crew was no fun. Apart from the obvious danger of attack by aircraft and depth charges, the main drawbacks were extremely cramped quarters, poor food and the all-pervading damp and oil. Every available space was used for storing supplies and torpedoes. Fresh water was reserved for cooking, and despite the best efforts of the men, clothes and bodies became filthy.

Every U-boat had a number and emblem. The flower is the edelweiss blossom, which was the emblem of submarine number U-124. The devil belonged to U-552.

U-boats were hunted by Allied warships using a system called sonar. It emitted a series of "pings" and listened for the echoes, which indicated the position of any underwater object.

Water tanks fore and aft (above) were used to adjust the U-boat's position in the sea by pumping water between them.

Aft torpedo room

Electric engine

Diesel engine

Anti-aircraft gun

Observation periscope

Gun for attacking ships

Conning tower

Control room

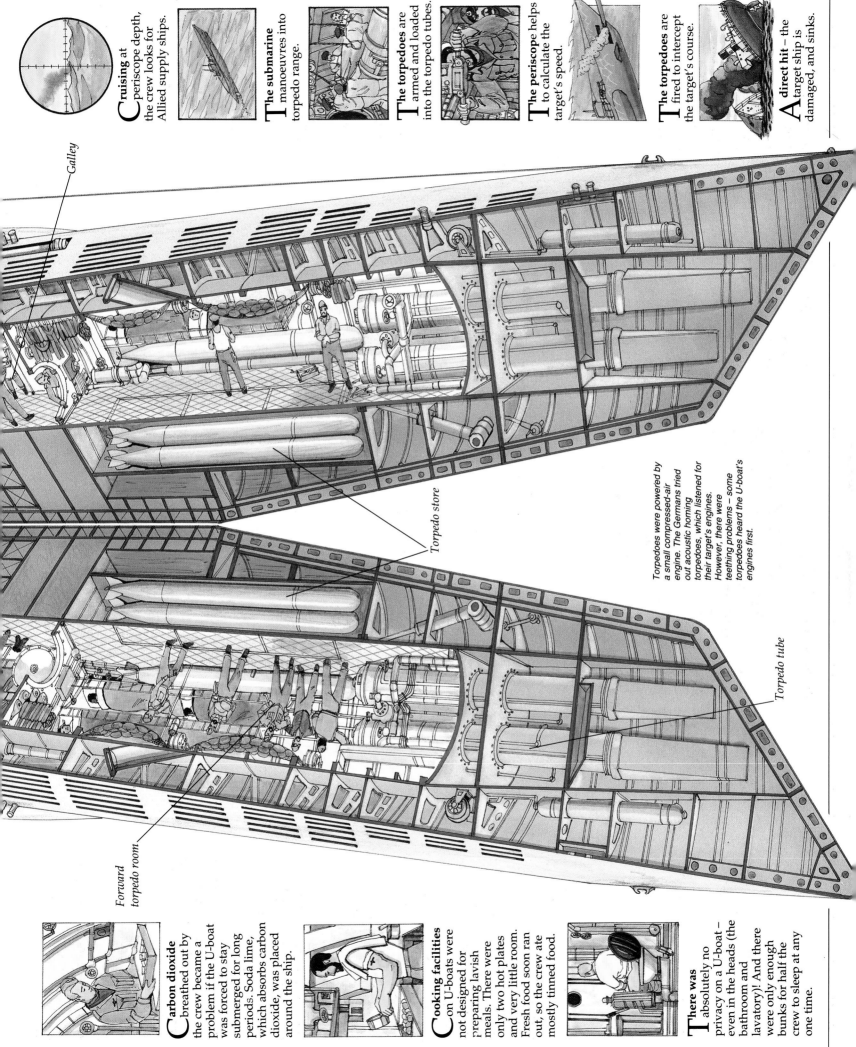

Cruising at periscope depth, the crew looks for Allied supply ships.

The submarine manoeuvres into torpedo range.

The torpedoes are armed and loaded into the torpedo tubes.

The periscope helps to calculate the target's speed.

The torpedoes are fired to intercept the target's course.

A direct hit – the target ship is damaged, and sinks.

Galley

Torpedo store

Forward torpedo room

Torpedo tube

Torpedoes were powered by a small compressed-air engine. The Germans tried out acoustic homing torpedoes, which listened for their target's engines. However, there were teething problems – some torpedoes heard the U-boat's engines first.

Carbon dioxide breathed out by the crew became a problem if the U-boat was forced to stay submerged for long periods. Soda lime, which absorbs carbon dioxide, was placed around the ship.

Cooking facilities on U-boats were not designed for preparing lavish meals. There were only two hot plates and very little room. Fresh food soon ran out, so the crew ate mostly tinned food.

There was absolutely no privacy on a U-boat – even in the heads (the bathroom and lavatory)! And there were only enough bunks for half the crew to sleep at any one time.

Cornelius Drebbel's machine (1620) was propelled by oars sticking out through leather flaps – water leaked through the flaps when it dived.

Bushnell (above) operated *Turtle* (1776) using hand cranks and foot pedals.

Resurgam (left) (1879) built up a head of steam on the surface before diving with the boiler fires extinguished.

Argonaut (below) (1894) was a diving bell which was intended to roll along the sea bed.

Nautilus (1800) could dive to a depth of 7.5 metres. When it was on the surface, auxiliary power came from a collapsible sail.

Ramming with an explosive charge mounted on the end of a pole was the American Civil War "David" submarine's method of attack in 1861.

THE HISTORY OF
Submarines

THE OLDEST SUBMARINE that we know actually existed was built c.1620, although ideas for submerged craft date from the third century BC, the time of the Ancient Greeks. That first submarine was built by Dutchman Cornelius Drebbel. It was a wooden craft covered in greased leather, and was tested in the River Thames in England. The first great step forwards in design was made by American engineer David Bushnell, whose *Turtle* dived and surfaced by filling ballast tanks with water, then emptying them. The first submarine to sink a ship was a "David"-type submarine, used by the Confederates in the American Civil War. The big problem was propulsion. Steam, petrol and diesel engines, which relied on burning fuel, were all right on the surface, but underwater they used up the air supply and filled the submarine with fumes. The answer was an electric motor. The American J P Holland combined petrol and electric propulsion for the first time in 1900.

A British navy "Holland" type submarine (left) (1901). It had petrol and electric engines. Mice were carried in early submarines to warn the crew when the air became unbreathable.

A typical U-boat of World War One (below). Torpedoes were fired from four tubes (two in the bow and two in the stern). The first German U-boat (number U1) was completed in 1906.

When there were no naval escorts to protect a ship, U-boats often attacked while surfaced, using a deck gun (a 10.5cm calibre in this case).

U-boats spent most of their time on the surface, travelling under diesel power. They could only travel about 130 km submerged.

Deck gun

Conning tower

Control room

Crew's quarters

Torpedo tubes were kept loaded all the time. In the early U-boats, torpedoes were precious because only about a dozen could be carried at a time.

Torpedo

Torpedo tube

24

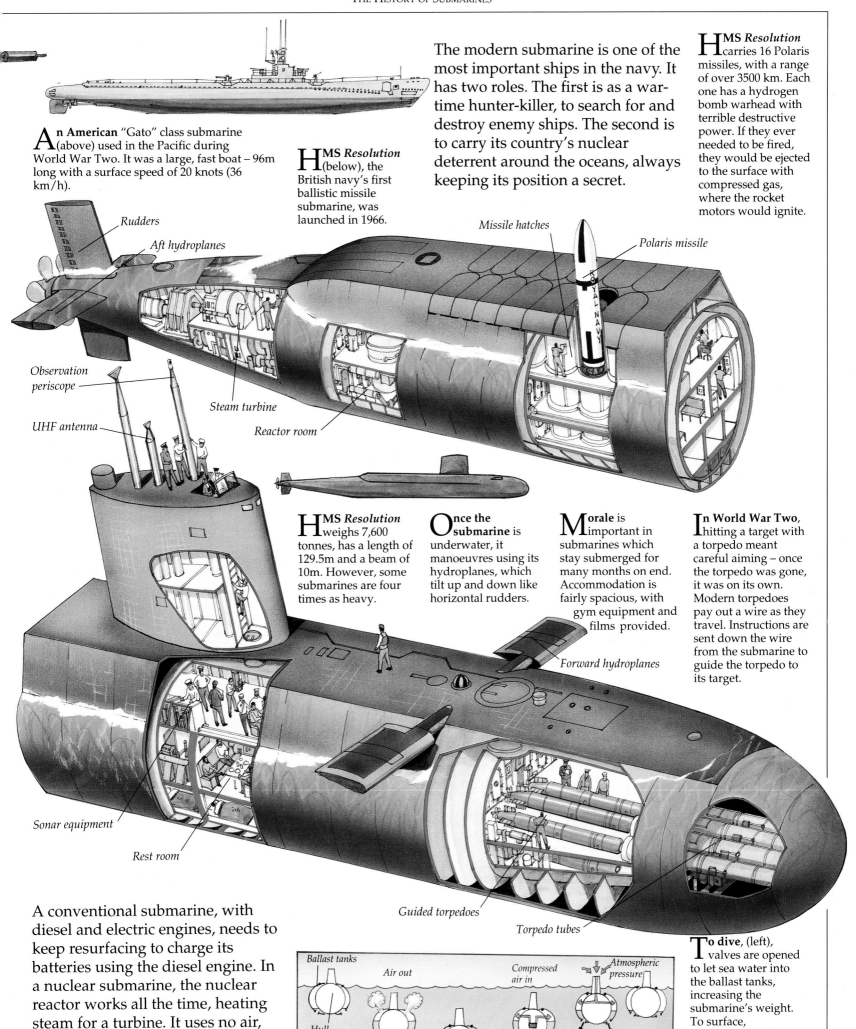

An American "Gato" class submarine (above) used in the Pacific during World War Two. It was a large, fast boat – 96m long with a surface speed of 20 knots (36 km/h).

The modern submarine is one of the most important ships in the navy. It has two roles. The first is as a war-time hunter-killer, to search for and destroy enemy ships. The second is to carry its country's nuclear deterrent around the oceans, always keeping its position a secret.

HMS *Resolution* (below), the British navy's first ballistic missile submarine, was launched in 1966.

HMS *Resolution* carries 16 Polaris missiles, with a range of over 3500 km. Each one has a hydrogen bomb warhead with terrible destructive power. If they ever needed to be fired, they would be ejected to the surface with compressed gas, where the rocket motors would ignite.

Rudders

Aft hydroplanes

Missile hatches

Polaris missile

Observation periscope

Steam turbine

Reactor room

UHF antenna

HMS *Resolution* weighs 7,600 tonnes, has a length of 129.5m and a beam of 10m. However, some submarines are four times as heavy.

Once the submarine is underwater, it manoeuvres using its hydroplanes, which tilt up and down like horizontal rudders.

Morale is important in submarines which stay submerged for many months on end. Accommodation is fairly spacious, with gym equipment and films provided.

In World War Two, hitting a target with a torpedo meant careful aiming – once the torpedo was gone, it was on its own. Modern torpedoes pay out a wire as they travel. Instructions are sent down the wire from the submarine to guide the torpedo to its target.

Forward hydroplanes

Sonar equipment

Rest room

Guided torpedoes

Torpedo tubes

A conventional submarine, with diesel and electric engines, needs to keep resurfacing to charge its batteries using the diesel engine. In a nuclear submarine, the nuclear reactor works all the time, heating steam for a turbine. It uses no air, makes no fumes and needs refuelling only every two years.

To dive, (left), valves are opened to let sea water into the ballast tanks, increasing the submarine's weight. To surface, compressed air is blown into the tanks to expel the water.

Ballast tanks

Air out

Compressed air in

Atmospheric pressure

Hull

Water in

Water out

THE GREAT AIRSHIPS

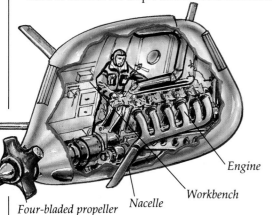

The outlined portion represents the part of the airship illustrated in the main X-ray picture below. On the rear section of the airship were fins and a tailplane, on which were mounted rudders and elevators. They were used to control the ship's altitude and direction.

Engine

Workbench

Four-bladed propeller *Nacelle*

Each of the four engines (above) was contained in a pod called a nacelle mounted alongside the hull. In each nacelle there was room for the engine itself, and for a flight engineer and a workbench. A door in the nacelle led to a gangway and door in the hull. Each Daimler diesel engine produced 1,000 horsepower, giving a top speed of 130 km/h.

AIRSHIPS WERE THE GIANTS OF THE SKY. The two biggest were the *Hindenburg* (245 metres long) and the *Graf Zeppelin* (236 metres long). They would have dwarfed the largest aircraft of today. Construction of the *Hindenburg* (or LZ129) began in 1934 in Germany and it made its maiden flight in March 1936. Seventy-five passengers could cross the Atlantic in style in just over two days. Travelling by airship became fashionable in the 1930s, although it was expensive and only a small number of passengers could be carried at a time. Massive airships crossed the Atlantic in half the time it took the great ocean liners, and with equal comfort for the first-class passengers.

A leaking gas bag and a spark from static electricity probably caused the fire which destroyed the *Hindenburg*. 35 of the 97 people on board were killed.

The control gondola and the engines were the only parts of the airship to break its streamlined surface. The passenger accommodation, which included cabins, a dining saloon, a reading and writing room and a lounge, was inside the hull. Passengers could look out through large windows on the promenade deck.

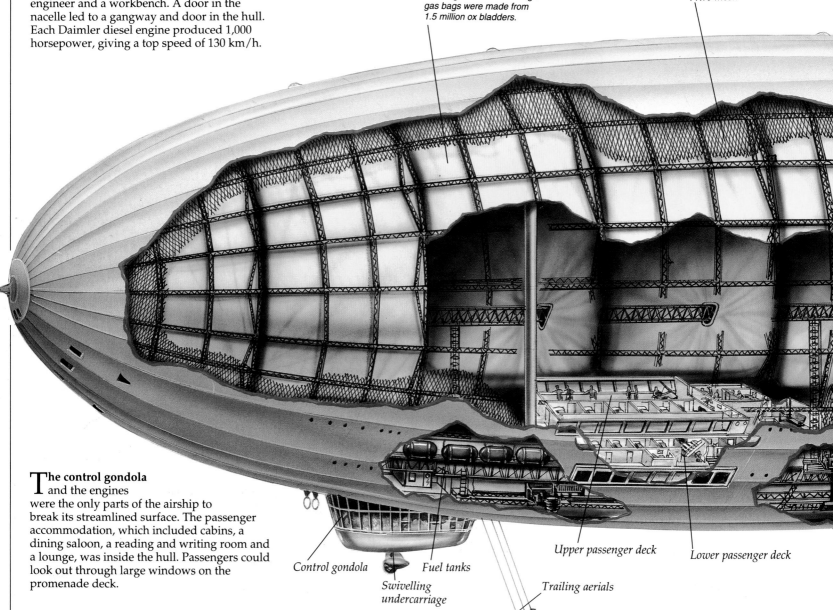

Gas bags. The Hindenburg's gas bags were made from 1.5 million ox bladders.

Wire mesh

Control gondola *Fuel tanks*

Swivelling undercarriage

Trailing aerials

Upper passenger deck *Lower passenger deck*

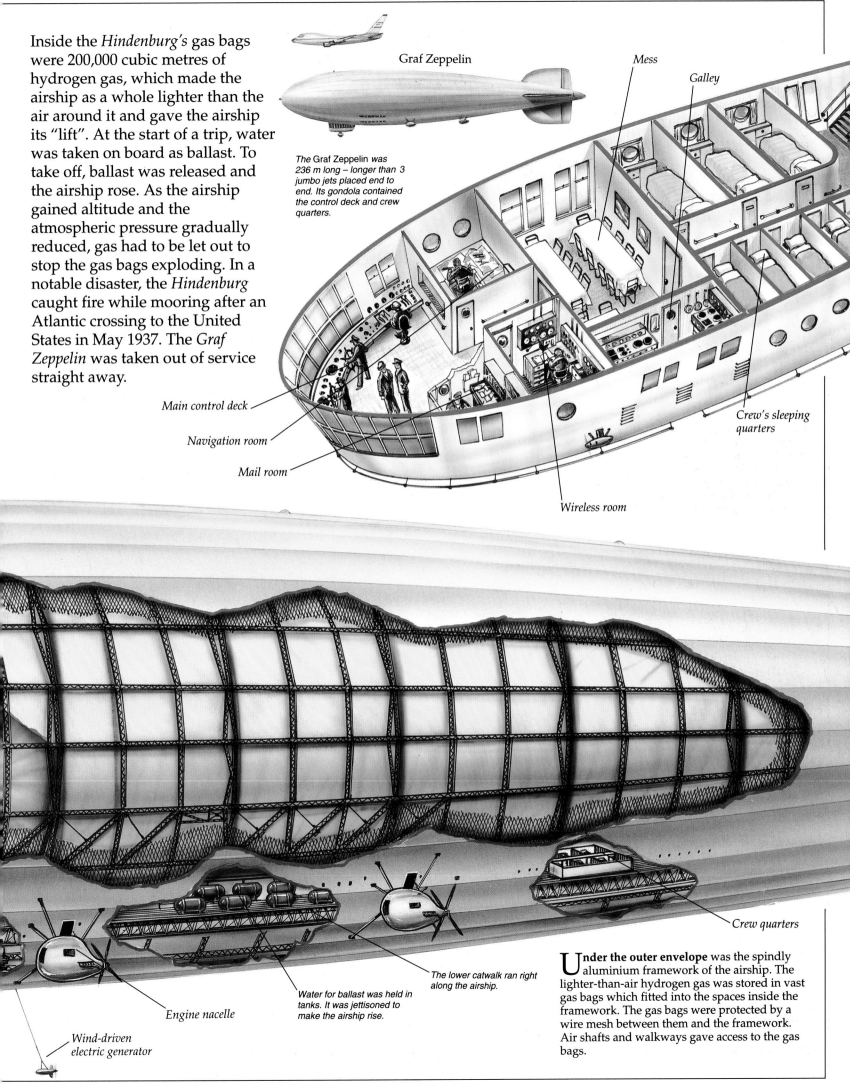

Inside the *Hindenburg's* gas bags were 200,000 cubic metres of hydrogen gas, which made the airship as a whole lighter than the air around it and gave the airship its "lift". At the start of a trip, water was taken on board as ballast. To take off, ballast was released and the airship rose. As the airship gained altitude and the atmospheric pressure gradually reduced, gas had to be let out to stop the gas bags exploding. In a notable disaster, the *Hindenburg* caught fire while mooring after an Atlantic crossing to the United States in May 1937. The *Graf Zeppelin* was taken out of service straight away.

Graf Zeppelin

The Graf Zeppelin was 236 m long – longer than 3 jumbo jets placed end to end. Its gondola contained the control deck and crew quarters.

Mess

Galley

Crew's sleeping quarters

Main control deck

Navigation room

Mail room

Wireless room

Engine nacelle

Wind-driven electric generator

Water for ballast was held in tanks. It was jettisoned to make the airship rise.

The lower catwalk ran right along the airship.

Crew quarters

Under the outer envelope was the spindly aluminium framework of the airship. The lighter-than-air hydrogen gas was stored in vast gas bags which fitted into the spaces inside the framework. The gas bags were protected by a wire mesh between them and the framework. Air shafts and walkways gave access to the gas bags.

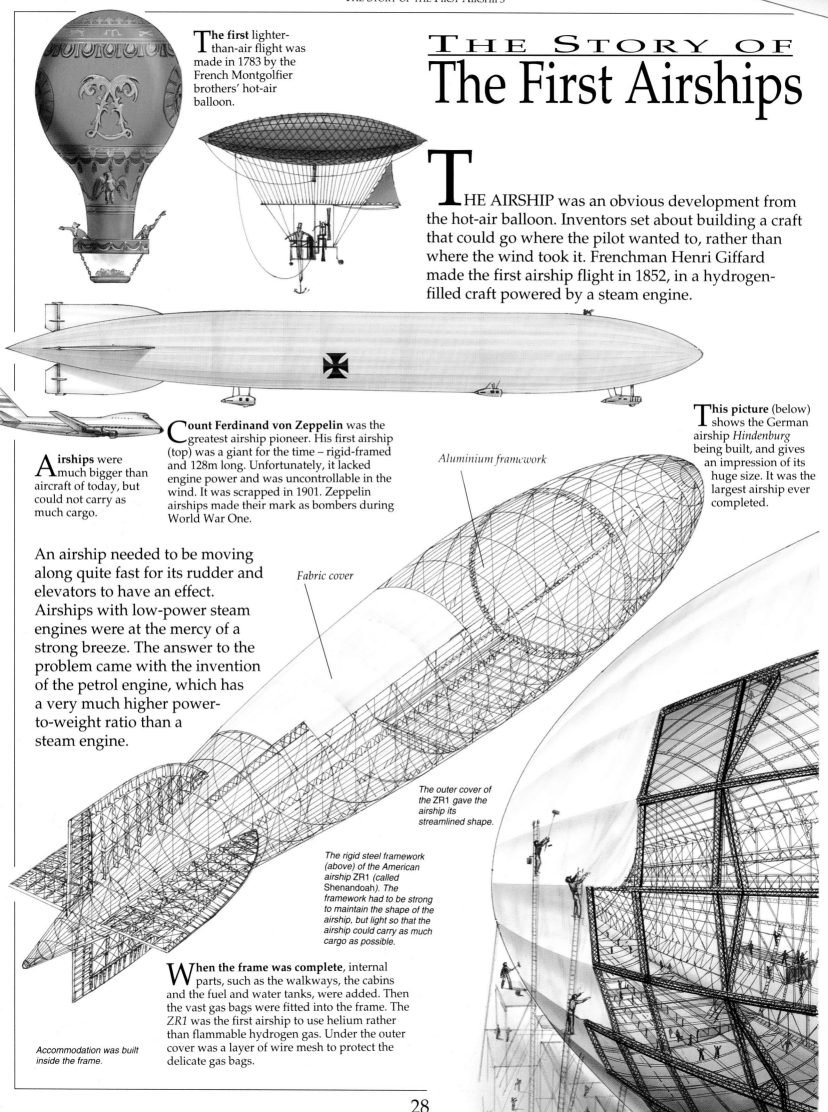

The first lighter-than-air flight was made in 1783 by the French Montgolfier brothers' hot-air balloon.

THE STORY OF
The First Airships

THE AIRSHIP was an obvious development from the hot-air balloon. Inventors set about building a craft that could go where the pilot wanted to, rather than where the wind took it. Frenchman Henri Giffard made the first airship flight in 1852, in a hydrogen-filled craft powered by a steam engine.

Airships were much bigger than aircraft of today, but could not carry as much cargo.

Count Ferdinand von Zeppelin was the greatest airship pioneer. His first airship (top) was a giant for the time – rigid-framed and 128m long. Unfortunately, it lacked engine power and was uncontrollable in the wind. It was scrapped in 1901. Zeppelin airships made their mark as bombers during World War One.

This picture (below) shows the German airship *Hindenburg* being built, and gives an impression of its huge size. It was the largest airship ever completed.

Aluminium framework

Fabric cover

An airship needed to be moving along quite fast for its rudder and elevators to have an effect. Airships with low-power steam engines were at the mercy of a strong breeze. The answer to the problem came with the invention of the petrol engine, which has a very much higher power-to-weight ratio than a steam engine.

The outer cover of the ZR1 gave the airship its streamlined shape.

The rigid steel framework (above) of the American airship ZR1 (called Shenandoah). The framework had to be strong to maintain the shape of the airship, but light so that the airship could carry as much cargo as possible.

Accommodation was built inside the frame.

When the frame was complete, internal parts, such as the walkways, the cabins and the fuel and water tanks, were added. Then the vast gas bags were fitted into the frame. The *ZR1* was the first airship to use helium rather than flammable hydrogen gas. Under the outer cover was a layer of wire mesh to protect the delicate gas bags.

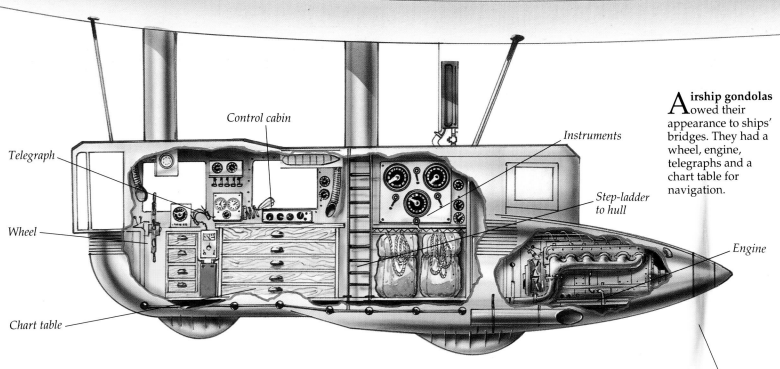

Telegraph

Control cabin

Instruments

Wheel

Step-ladder
to hull

Chart table

Engine

Propeller

Airship gondolas owed their appearance to ships' bridges. They had a wheel, engine, telegraphs and a chart table for navigation.

Airship design advanced rapidly in the ten years before World War One. Early airships had been non-rigid or semi-rigid – they were really just streamlined balloons. Both types kept their shape because the gas inside was under slight pressure. But any leak meant the shape was lost and the airship became difficult to fly. Designers realised that a rigid frame was one answer. The problem of extra weight was overcome by building big – the L70, a typical World War One German Zeppelin airship, was 211 metres long and 24 metres wide.

After the war, designers turned their attention to building passenger-carrying airships. The British *R100* and *R101* airships were even intended for use on a route all the way from England to India. However, after several fatal accidents, especially those of the British *R101* in France in 1930 and the German *Hindenburg* in 1937, people lost faith in airship travel. Today, small airships, typically about 60m long, are sometimes used as floating advertisements, or for aerial photography.

A typical forward gondola of a rigid airship (above). It hung underneath the frame, giving an all-round view of the ground below. Inside was the control cabin, from which the pilot flew the airship. A step-ladder led from the gondola into a hatch in the hull. Underneath was a landing skid in case of emergency landings.

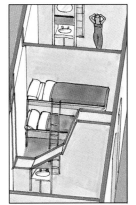

Passenger cabins were normally inside the hull.

Airships had no undercarriage. They had to be moored to the ground in some way to stop them drifting off in the wind, so special mooring posts were built.

The *Graf Zeppelin* (below) being towed from its vast hangar in Friedrichshaven in Germany in 1928.

Larger airships stopped at tall, purpose-built mooring posts. These kept the airship clear of the ground, which could damage the delicate gondolas if they were blown about by the wind. The post also allowed the airship to swivel, keeping its nose into the wind. The nose of the airship contained mooring lines which were fed out through hatches.

Swivel

Mooring post

The Graf Zeppelin, at 236m, was just 9 m shorter than the Hindenburg. Between its launch in 1928 and 1937, it made over 500 transatlantic flights, and was the first airship to circumnavigate the world.

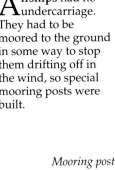

Hangar

Towing gantry

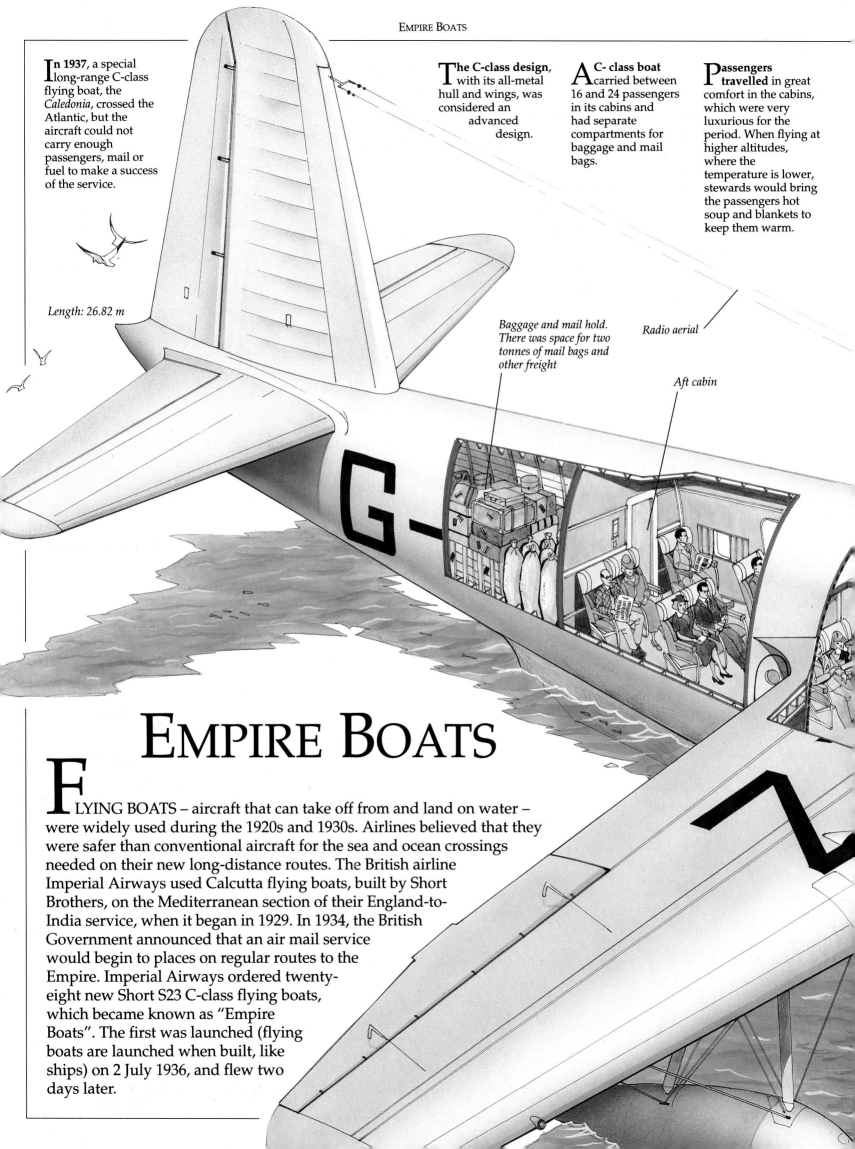

In 1937, a special long-range C-class flying boat, the *Caledonia*, crossed the Atlantic, but the aircraft could not carry enough passengers, mail or fuel to make a success of the service.

Length: 26.82 m

The C-class design, with its all-metal hull and wings, was considered an advanced design.

A C-class boat carried between 16 and 24 passengers in its cabins and had separate compartments for baggage and mail bags.

Passengers travelled in great comfort in the cabins, which were very luxurious for the period. When flying at higher altitudes, where the temperature is lower, stewards would bring the passengers hot soup and blankets to keep them warm.

Baggage and mail hold. There was space for two tonnes of mail bags and other freight

Radio aerial

Aft cabin

EMPIRE BOATS

FLYING BOATS – aircraft that can take off from and land on water – were widely used during the 1920s and 1930s. Airlines believed that they were safer than conventional aircraft for the sea and ocean crossings needed on their new long-distance routes. The British airline Imperial Airways used Calcutta flying boats, built by Short Brothers, on the Mediterranean section of their England-to-India service, when it began in 1929. In 1934, the British Government announced that an air mail service would begin to places on regular routes to the Empire. Imperial Airways ordered twenty-eight new Short S23 C-class flying boats, which became known as "Empire Boats". The first was launched (flying boats are launched when built, like ships) on 2 July 1936, and flew two days later.

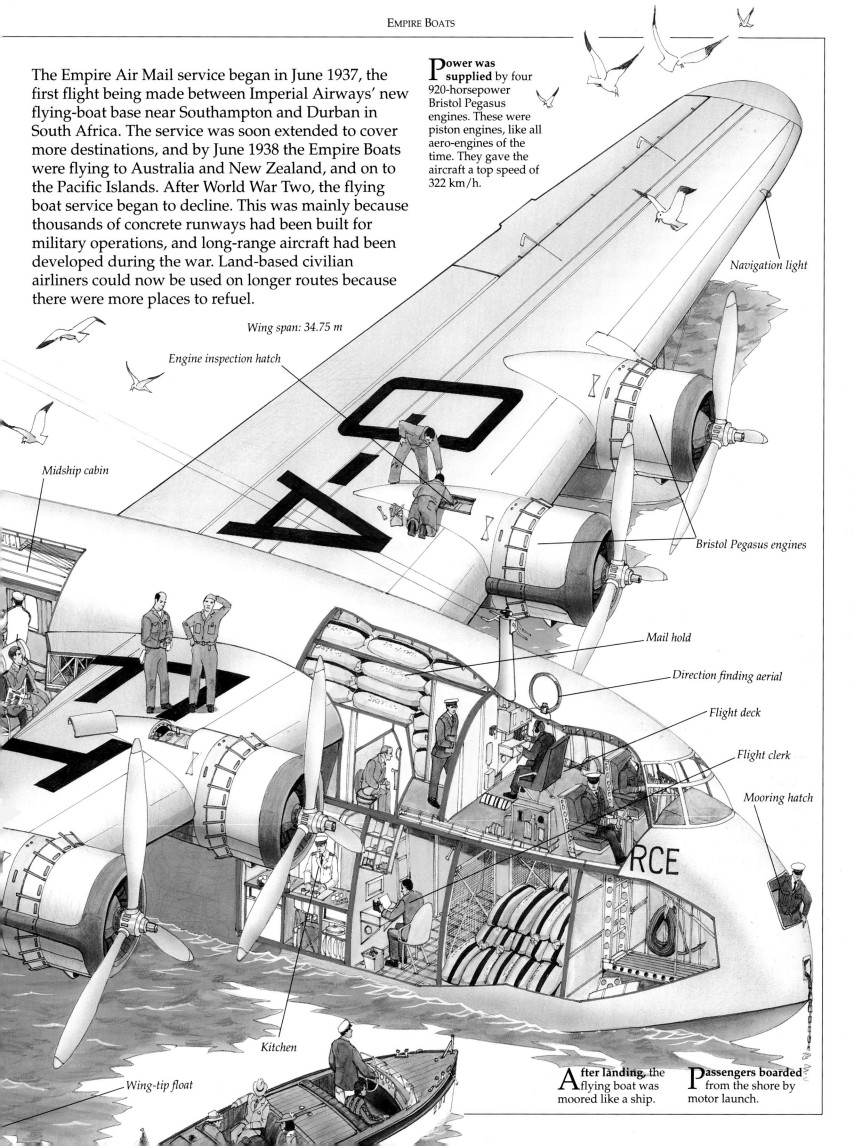

The Empire Air Mail service began in June 1937, the first flight being made between Imperial Airways' new flying-boat base near Southampton and Durban in South Africa. The service was soon extended to cover more destinations, and by June 1938 the Empire Boats were flying to Australia and New Zealand, and on to the Pacific Islands. After World War Two, the flying boat service began to decline. This was mainly because thousands of concrete runways had been built for military operations, and long-range aircraft had been developed during the war. Land-based civilian airliners could now be used on longer routes because there were more places to refuel.

Power was supplied by four 920-horsepower Bristol Pegasus engines. These were piston engines, like all aero-engines of the time. They gave the aircraft a top speed of 322 km/h.

Navigation light

Wing span: 34.75 m

Engine inspection hatch

Midship cabin

Bristol Pegasus engines

Mail hold

Direction finding aerial

Flight deck

Flight clerk

Mooring hatch

Kitchen

Wing-tip float

After landing, the flying boat was moored like a ship.

Passengers boarded from the shore by motor launch.

THE FIRST
Flying boats

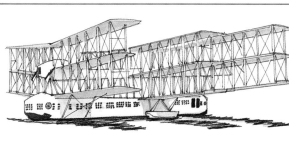

THE ADVANTAGES OF AN AIRCRAFT that could land on water were clear from the very start of aviation history. Water was smoother to land on than a rough field and could provide a runway of unlimited length. Also, sea crossings could be made in greater safety because the aircraft could land if the engine failed (provided the sea was not too rough). The first take-off from water was made by Frenchman Henri Fabre in March 1910, in an aircraft with a float where the undercarriage would normally have been. Many early aviators built and flew these "floatplanes". Eventually, a distinction was made between small aircraft with floats under the fuselage, known as floatplanes, and aircraft with a hull-shaped fuselage, known as flying boats. The first successful flying boat, named the *Flying Fish*, was built in early 1912 by American Glen Curtiss.

Pan American was the first airline to offer a transatlantic service.

Lack of range was a problem for early airliners. One experiment tried by Imperial Airways was to carry a seaplane to its cruising height on "piggy back" (below). The smaller aircraft then started its flight with a full load of fuel, and could fly much further.

The bizarre Italian Caproni Ca 60 Transaereo (above) was designed to be the first airliner to carry 100 passengers across the Atlantic. The triple triplane crashed on its maiden flight in 1921.

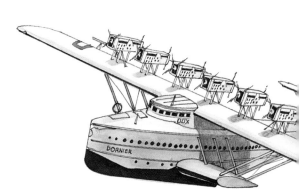

The massive German Dornier Do X of 1929, with its twelve engines, was a commercial failure.

Imperial Airways' route from England to Singapore. The journey took 5½ days.

From Singapore, there was a service to Australia and on to the Pacific Islands.

At British Imperial Airways' own special flying boat terminal near Southampton, passengers boarded their flight at the jetty.

The meals served on the Empire Boats rivalled those available in top hotels. They were freshly cooked and served by a steward.

In the evening, the day-cabins were converted to bedrooms and the passengers slept as the plane flew on through the night.

After 5 days' flying time, and having changed planes a few times, the passengers finally arrived in Singapore harbour.

Near the end of World War One, flying boats proved their military value by making successful attacks on U-boats, but they really made their mark after the war by opening up the world's air routes. Like conventional aircraft of the time, they could not fly long distances, but they had the advantage of being able to land and refuel at any port, large or small. Conventional aircraft of the same size needed a specially built landing strip, and there were very few of those before World War Two. International airlines soon began to use flying boats on the over-water sections of their routes. In the late 1930s, flying boats were the fastest way to travel across the world.

The Short Sunderland (above) was based on the Short C-class flying boat. It did a variety of war-time jobs, including anti-submarine warfare.

Submarines were located by radar (the aerials are on the rear of the hull) and attacked with bombs and depth charges.

Boeing's model 314 *Yankee Clipper* (above) had luxury cabins for its passengers.

The flight deck on the upper deck of the *Yankee Clipper* was the biggest ever built.

The Hughes H4 only flew once, in 1947, for less than 1 km, piloted by Hughes himself.

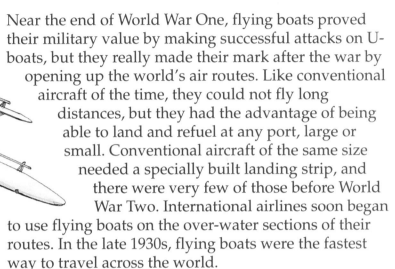

Multi-millionaire Howard Hughes built the largest flying boat ever — the Hughes H4 *Spruce Goose* (right). It was designed to carry up to 750 passengers.

The H4's wingspan of 97.51m is the longest of any aircraft ever built.

NX37502

BOEING 747

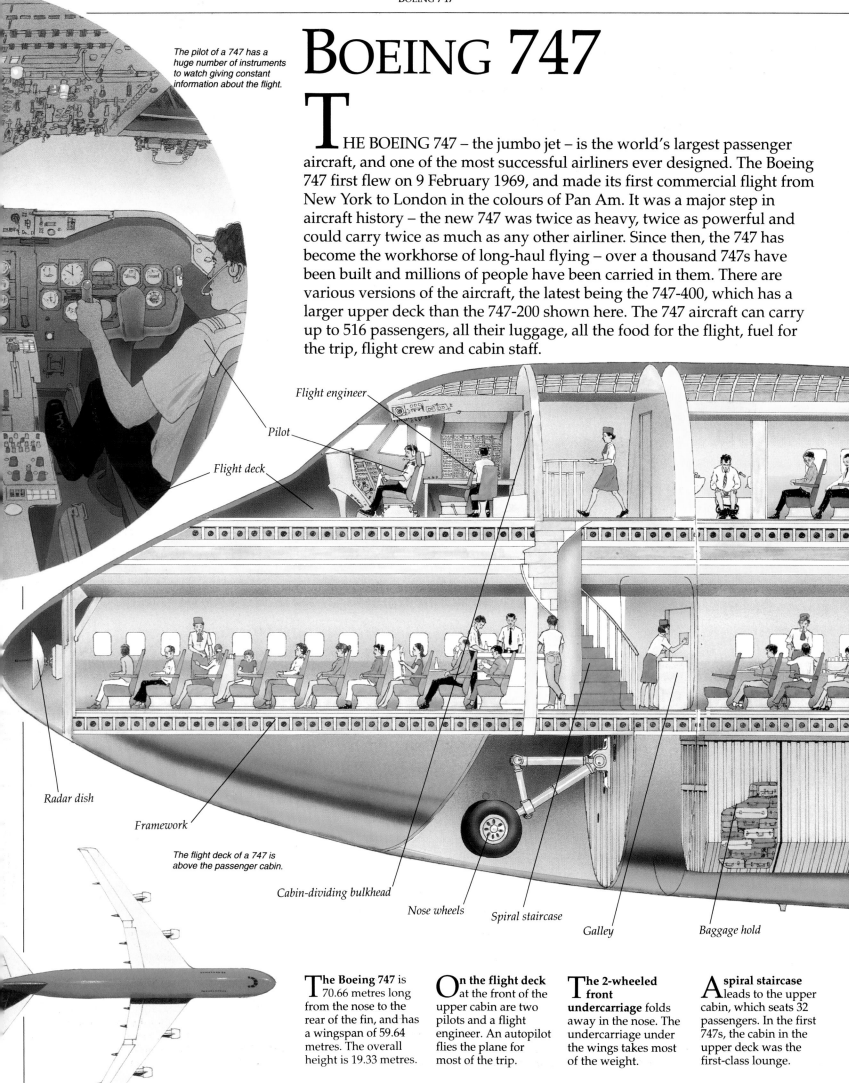

The pilot of a 747 has a huge number of instruments to watch giving constant information about the flight.

THE BOEING 747 – the jumbo jet – is the world's largest passenger aircraft, and one of the most successful airliners ever designed. The Boeing 747 first flew on 9 February 1969, and made its first commercial flight from New York to London in the colours of Pan Am. It was a major step in aircraft history – the new 747 was twice as heavy, twice as powerful and could carry twice as much as any other airliner. Since then, the 747 has become the workhorse of long-haul flying – over a thousand 747s have been built and millions of people have been carried in them. There are various versions of the aircraft, the latest being the 747-400, which has a larger upper deck than the 747-200 shown here. The 747 aircraft can carry up to 516 passengers, all their luggage, all the food for the flight, fuel for the trip, flight crew and cabin staff.

Flight engineer

Pilot

Flight deck

Radar dish

Framework

The flight deck of a 747 is above the passenger cabin.

Cabin-dividing bulkhead

Nose wheels

Spiral staircase

Galley

Baggage hold

The Boeing 747 is 70.66 metres long from the nose to the rear of the fin, and has a wingspan of 59.64 metres. The overall height is 19.33 metres.

On the flight deck at the front of the upper cabin are two pilots and a flight engineer. An autopilot flies the plane for most of the trip.

The 2-wheeled front undercarriage folds away in the nose. The undercarriage under the wings takes most of the weight.

A spiral staircase leads to the upper cabin, which seats 32 passengers. In the first 747s, the cabin in the upper deck was the first-class lounge.

Despite its immense size, the Boeing 747 has a reputation among airline pilots as being easy to fly, and it has a good safety record. Along the rear edges of the wings, and in the tailplanes and fin, are hydraulically powered control surfaces. The engines are contained in pods attached to the wings with pylons, which are designed to break if an engine seizes up. The tail section contains a small gas turbine engine, which provides power for the aircraft's electrical systems while it is on the ground.

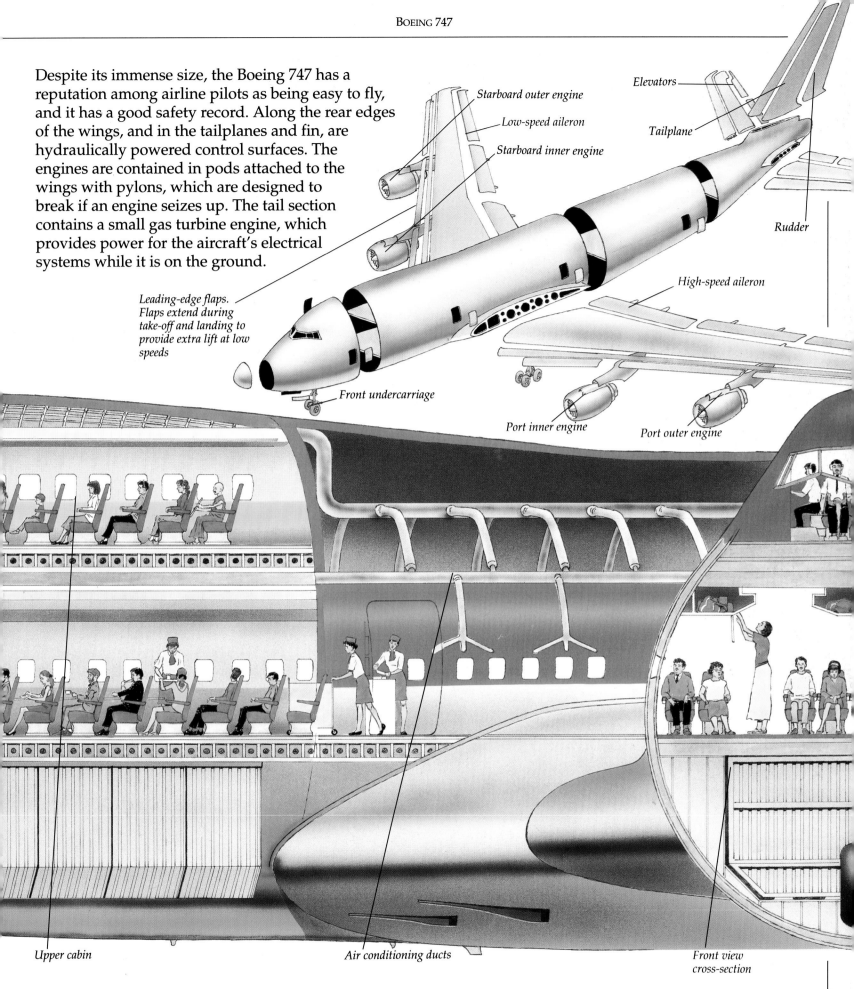

Starboard outer engine

Low-speed aileron

Starboard inner engine

Elevators

Tailplane

Rudder

High-speed aileron

Leading-edge flaps. Flaps extend during take-off and landing to provide extra lift at low speeds

Front undercarriage

Port inner engine

Port outer engine

Upper cabin

Air conditioning ducts

Front view cross-section

Passengers' bags and cases are loaded into containers in the airport, and the containers are loaded into the hold, under the passenger cabin.

The ten cabin doors slot into their frames from inside, like plugs. In flight, the air pressure in the cabin pushes on them, creating a tight fit.

Meals (there might be three on a long-haul flight) are prepared before the flight and heated up in the galley before being served.

The passenger cabin is pressurised with air for the passengers to breathe. Emergency oxygen is there in case the pressure is lost.

The 747SP long-range jumbo jet flies the world's longest non-stop route, the 12,050-km, 15-hour trip from Los Angeles to Sydney.

The fuselage is built from aluminium alloy, which is much lighter than steel. The thin outer skin is supported by an inner framework.

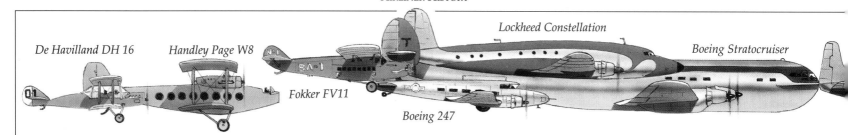

De Havilland DH 16

Handley Page W8

Fokker FV11

Lockheed Constellation

Boeing 247

Boeing Stratocruiser

De Havilland DH 16 (1918). The four-seat airliner was adapted from a World War One bomber, the de Havilland DH 9. It cruised at 160 km/h.

Handley Page W8 (1919). The W8 was based on another Handley Page aircraft, the O/400, a World War One bomber. It had 12 or 14 seats.

Fokker FVII (1923). The 3-engined version carried 8–10 passengers, and was one of the most popular airliners of the late 1920s.

Boeing 247 (1933). This all-metal, 10-seat airliner had retractable undercarriage, and was the forerunner of the modern airliner.

Lockheed Constellation (1943). This was the first airliner with a pressurised cabin, which meant it could fly above bad weather.

Boeing Stratocruiser (1946). Used mainly for first-class transatlantic services, it had 100 seats and a lounge and bar.

World War One was responsible for a huge expansion in the aircraft industry, and passenger flights began soon after hostilities ceased. The first regular international flight, between Paris and Brussels, started in 1919. But it was not until the 1930s and the introduction of larger, more comfortable aircraft that air travel really expanded. The real breakthrough was the jet airliner, which was fast and comfortable, and opened air travel to ordinary people.

AIRLINER HISTORY AND
Building the Jumbo

THE JUMBO JET was designed to answer the airlines' need for efficiency. They wanted an aircraft that could make fewer flights to move the same number of passengers. With a full load of passengers and all the fuel for a long flight, the 747 weighs 340 tonnes. At this weight, it needs over three kilometres of runway to reach its take-off speed. The fuel tanks, which are built into the wings, can hold over 200,000 litres of aviation fuel. At cruising speed (920 km/h), the four turbofan engines consume over 200 litres of fuel between them every minute. The aircraft has a range of between 11,000 and 12,000 kilometres, depending on the type of engines and number of passengers it carries.

Tailplane

The wings are hollow and contain the fuel

Pylons hold engines under wing

Regular maintenance is a vital factor in airline safety

The 747's huge undercarriage consists of 18 landing wheels: 4 groups of 4 wheels under the wings, and 2 under the nose. The air in the tyres is at very high pressure to take the force of 250 tonnes as the plane lands.

When the plane is on the ground, the pilots are 9 metres above the wheels.

Caravelle

Concorde

Viscount

Boeing 707

Boeing 747

McDonnell Douglas MD-11

Vickers-Armstrong **Viscount** (1953). The Viscount used turbo-prop engines; much more powerful and much quieter than piston engines.

Sud-Aviation **Caravelle** (1955). The French twin-engined Caravelle was one of the first jet-powered airliners in the world.

Boeing 707 (1958). The first of the big jet airliners. It could carry up to 179 passengers at a cruising speed of 917 km/h.

Boeing 747 (1970). This was the first wide-bodied jet to go into service, with two decks and seats for more than 500 passengers.

Concorde (1976). The Anglo-French Concorde was the first supersonic airliner. It has a cruising speed of 2,143 km/h – twice the speed of sound.

McDonnell **Douglas MD-11** (1986). It features an electronic flight deck, and uses high-tech materials like carbon-fibre and kevlar.

Several models of the Boeing 747 have been built. There are passenger versions, freighters, and combined passenger/freight planes (called combis). Customers who buy 747s have a choice of engine makes and seating arrangements, depending on their requirements for carrying capacity and range. The latest model, the 747-400, has new features which improve its range and efficiency. Small winglets at the wing tips increase the range by about three per cent. On the flight deck, the traditional instruments have been replaced by digital avionics, which are used on most modern airliners. The numerous gauges, dials and lights have gone, and in their place are computer monitors which display all the information needed by the pilot. The pilot can even programme the computers to fly the plane automatically all the way from take-off to landing.

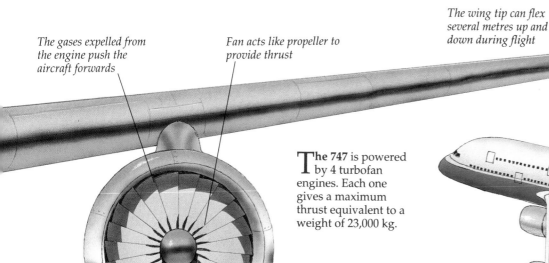

Boeing 747s, like other airliners, are built in sections which are assembled in huge sheds. Various parts of the aircraft are built by different sub-contractors.

With the aircraft structure complete, internal systems, such as electronics and hydraulics, are added. The completed aircraft is test-flown thoroughly.

Safety is a vital factor in aircraft design. The structure and control systems are designed to be "fail safe", so that if something goes wrong, there is always a back-up.

The wing tip can flex several metres up and down during flight

The gases expelled from the engine push the aircraft forwards

Fan acts like propeller to provide thrust

The 747 is powered by 4 turbofan engines. Each one gives a maximum thrust equivalent to a weight of 23,000 kg.

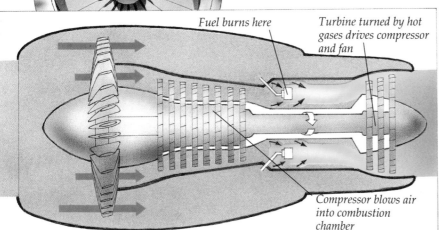

Fuel burns here

Turbine turned by hot gases drives compressor and fan

Compressor blows air into combustion chamber

The Boeing 747 design is so good that planes are still being built over twenty years after the first one flew. On the drawing board at Boeing are plans for the biggest plane of all time, a "super jumbo" with two decks and seats for 1000 passengers. It would be able to make longer non-stop flights than ever before.

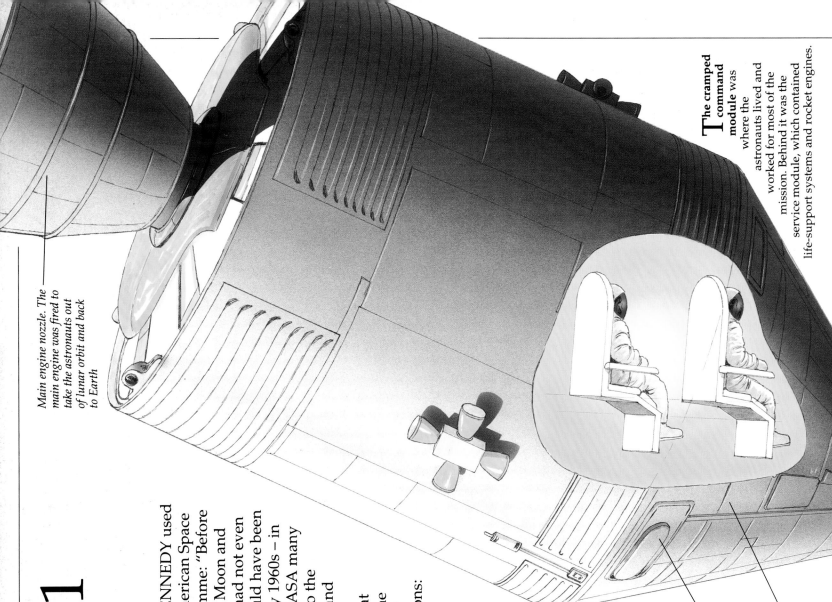

Main engine nozzle. The main engine was fired to take the astronauts out of lunar orbit and back to Earth

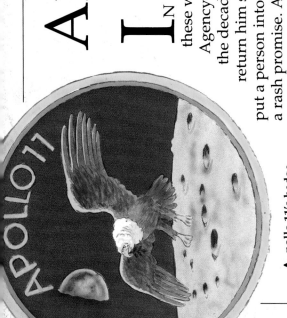

APOLLO 11

IN 1961 PRESIDENT JOHN F KENNEDY used these words to launch the North American Space Agency's (NASA) Moon-shot programme: "Before the decade is out, to land a man on the Moon and return him safely to Earth." As America had not even put a person into Earth orbit at that time, it could have been a rash promise. A series of missions in the early 1960s – in the Mercury and Gemini spacecraft – taught NASA many of the technical skills needed for the long trip to the Moon, which would require several dockings and faultless rocket firings. NASA then set about designing a completely new spacecraft, one that would be able to travel to the Moon, land on the surface, lift off again and return to Earth. Their solution was Apollo. It consisted of three sections: the command module, the service module and the lunar module, and it would carry three astronauts, two of whom would land on the Moon. There were a series of Apollo missions to test the new spacecraft, each going one step further towards the ultimate goal. Apollos 5 and 6 went into space unmanned. Apollo 7 took astronauts into Earth orbit, and Apollo 8 took them into lunar orbit. The lunar module was tested by missions 9 and 10. On 20 July 1969 the lunar module of Apollo 11 touched down on the Moon, and nearly six hours later, Neil Armstrong stepped onto the lunar surface. There were still five months left of the 1960s, so President Kennedy's promise was fulfilled.

Docking window, which the astronauts looked through to line up the command and lunar modules for docking

Command module

The cramped command module was where the astronauts lived and worked for most of the mission. Behind it was the service module, which contained life-support systems and rocket engines.

Apollo 11's badge showed an eagle (the lunar module was called Eagle) carrying an olive branch (the symbol of peace). The message "The Eagle has landed" caused great excitement.

The most famous astronaut of all, Neil Armstrong, the first man to walk on the Moon. Armstrong got his pilot's licence on his 16th birthday, flew for the US Navy and was a NASA test pilot.

The lunar module was seven metres high and weighed 14 tonnes. It had two sections. The descent stage contained a rocket engine, which would slow down the module and ensure a soft landing, and also the landing legs, which had to unfold before the Moon landing. The astronauts travelled in the ascent stage. It contained another rocket engine for leaving the Moon, and used the descent stage as a take-off pad. Armstrong and Aldrin climbed into the lunar module to descend to the lunar surface, leaving Collins in orbit in the command module. There was a limited amount of fuel for the descent engine, and there was only about twenty seconds' worth left when Armstrong finally landed the module on the surface. The most critical part of the mission followed twenty-two hours later. Armstrong fired the ascent engines to leave the Moon. Had the engine not worked, he and Aldrin would have been stuck – with no chance of rescue.

Manoeuvring engines on all three modules were used for docking and turning the spacecraft

Landing leg

Docking radar

Docking hatch

Exit hatch

Lunar module

Ascent stage

Descent stage

Edwin "Buzz" Aldrin landed on the Moon with Armstrong, and stepped onto it a few minutes after him. Aldrin was an expert on docking spacecraft in orbit.

The third member of the crew was Michael Collins. He stayed in orbit in the command module while the other two landed on the Moon. Collins was a former Air Force test pilot.

TRAVELLING TO
The Moon and Back

THE APOLLO 11 MISSION in 1969 (and the five other Moon shots that followed it) was an extremely complicated operation. It needed a series of spacecraft manoeuvres and dockings to work perfectly. As well as a new spacecraft, the Moon landing programme needed a rocket with much more lifting power than any in existence. In 1961, NASA began work on the Saturn V, and first tested it in 1967. It was a three-stage rocket, 111 metres high, weighed nearly 3000 tonnes full of fuel, and could carry 150 tonnes of equipment into space. The first stage had five engines, each of which burnt three tonnes of kerosene and liquid oxygen every second.

The Saturn V rocket had 3 stages (sections), each of which lifted the Apollo spacecraft further into space. The third stage rocket also fired Apollo out of Earth orbit towards the Moon.

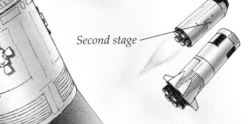

At a height of 65 km, the main engines shut down and the first stage separated.

The second stage engines took the rocket to 185 km high. The third stage put the spacecraft into orbit.

Escape tower

Command module

Second stage

Lunar module

Liquid hydrogen tank

Stage three engine

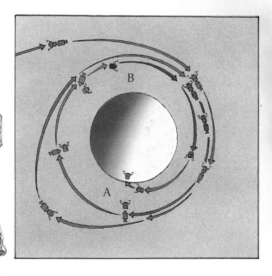

The diagram above shows how the Saturn V rocket entered lunar orbit and landed on the Moon. After orbiting the Moon one and a half times, the command and service modules detached from the lunar module (A), which began to turn in preparation for landing on the moon (B). The command and service modules stayed in orbit.

A foil collector caught minute particles from the Sun for later analysis.

The astronauts wore backpacks known as portable life-support systems (PLSS), which kept them cool and carried their oxygen supply.

During their time on the Moon, astronauts Armstrong and Aldrin set up a TV camera, raised the American flag (with a wire insert to hold it out from the pole), and gathered rock samples. They also set up several experiments, including a seismic unit to record lunar "earthquakes".

Among the items left on the Moon was a plaque signed by President Richard Nixon and the three astronauts.

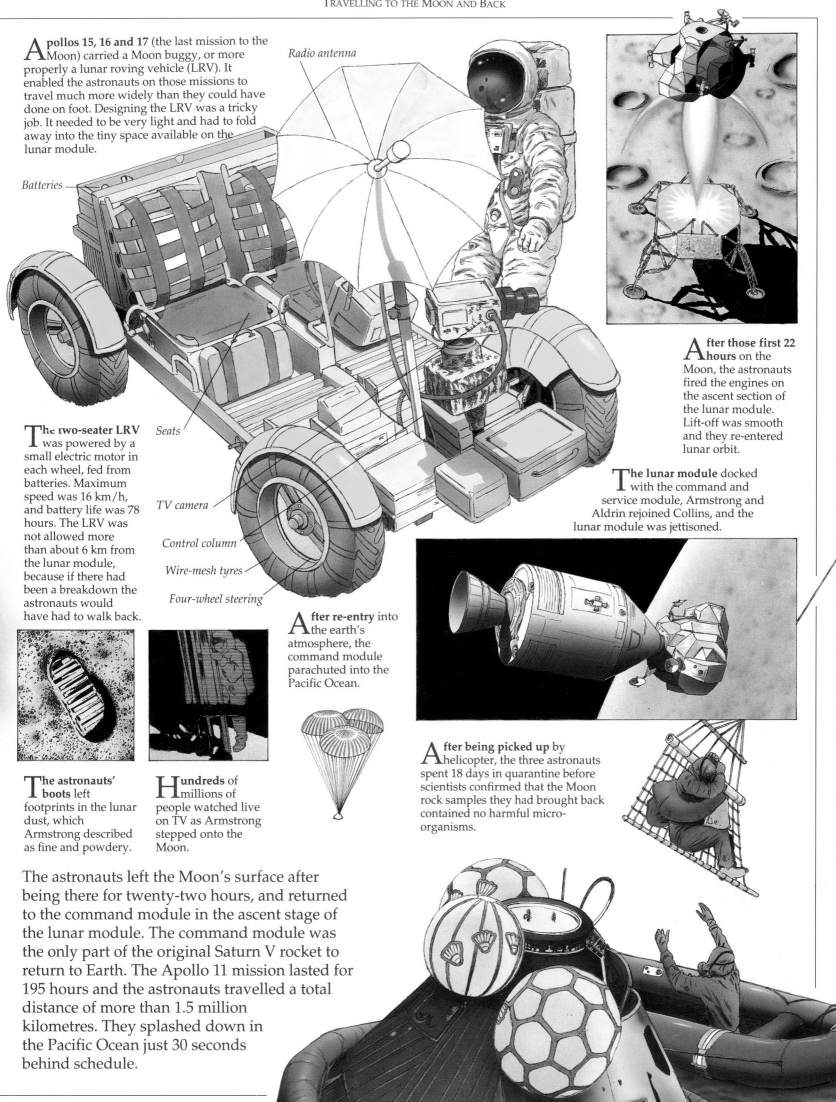

Apollos 15, 16 and 17 (the last mission to the Moon) carried a Moon buggy, or more properly a lunar roving vehicle (LRV). It enabled the astronauts on those missions to travel much more widely than they could have done on foot. Designing the LRV was a tricky job. It needed to be very light and had to fold away into the tiny space available on the lunar module.

Radio antenna

Batteries

The two-seater LRV was powered by a small electric motor in each wheel, fed from batteries. Maximum speed was 16 km/h, and battery life was 78 hours. The LRV was not allowed more than about 6 km from the lunar module, because if there had been a breakdown the astronauts would have had to walk back.

Seats

TV camera

Control column

Wire-mesh tyres

Four-wheel steering

The astronauts' boots left footprints in the lunar dust, which Armstrong described as fine and powdery.

Hundreds of millions of people watched live on TV as Armstrong stepped onto the Moon.

After re-entry into the earth's atmosphere, the command module parachuted into the Pacific Ocean.

After those first 22 hours on the Moon, the astronauts fired the engines on the ascent section of the lunar module. Lift-off was smooth and they re-entered lunar orbit.

The lunar module docked with the command and service module, Armstrong and Aldrin rejoined Collins, and the lunar module was jettisoned.

After being picked up by helicopter, the three astronauts spent 18 days in quarantine before scientists confirmed that the Moon rock samples they had brought back contained no harmful micro-organisms.

The astronauts left the Moon's surface after being there for twenty-two hours, and returned to the command module in the ascent stage of the lunar module. The command module was the only part of the original Saturn V rocket to return to Earth. The Apollo 11 mission lasted for 195 hours and the astronauts travelled a total distance of more than 1.5 million kilometres. They splashed down in the Pacific Ocean just 30 seconds behind schedule.

THE SPACE SHUTTLE

The aircraft-like part of the Shuttle is called the orbiter. It is the only part that actually goes into orbit.

Getting into space by rocket is an expensive business. To put even a small satellite into orbit, you need a big rocket to launch it, and you never see the rocket again. The United States' answer to the problem was to develop the Space Shuttle, the world's first re-usable launch vehicle. The Shuttle is part spacecraft, part aircraft. It launches like a rocket, orbits in space during its mission and glides back to Earth.

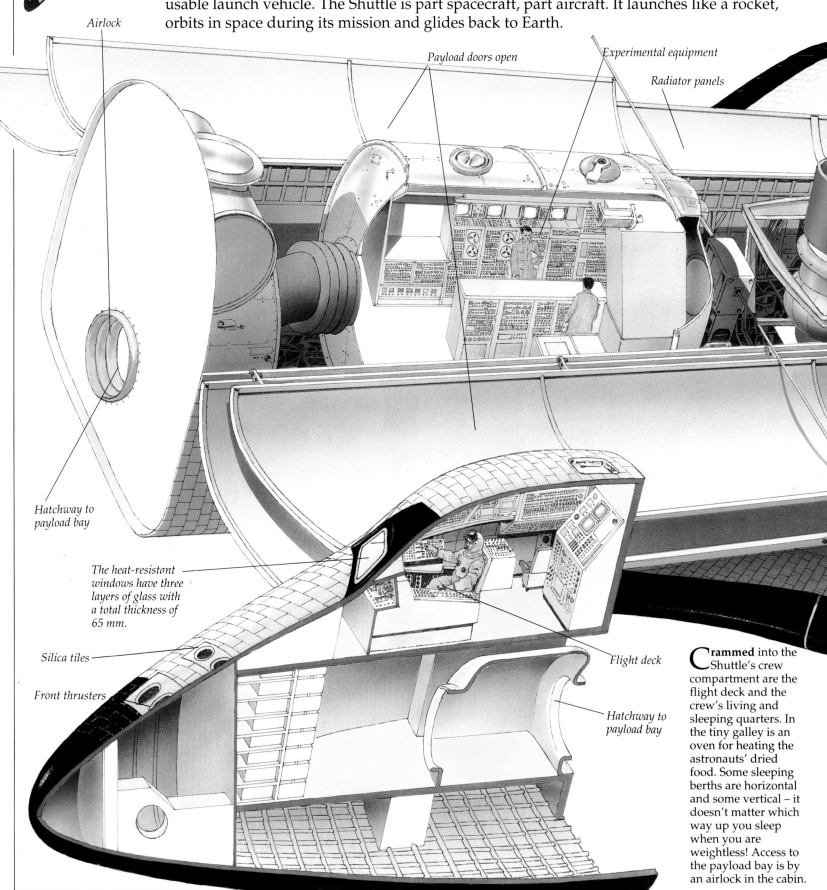

Airlock

Payload doors open

Experimental equipment

Radiator panels

Hatchway to payload bay

The heat-resistant windows have three layers of glass with a total thickness of 65 mm.

Silica tiles

Front thrusters

Flight deck

Hatchway to payload bay

Crammed into the Shuttle's crew compartment are the flight deck and the crew's living and sleeping quarters. In the tiny galley is an oven for heating the astronauts' dried food. Some sleeping berths are horizontal and some vertical – it doesn't matter which way up you sleep when you are weightless! Access to the payload bay is by an airlock in the cabin.

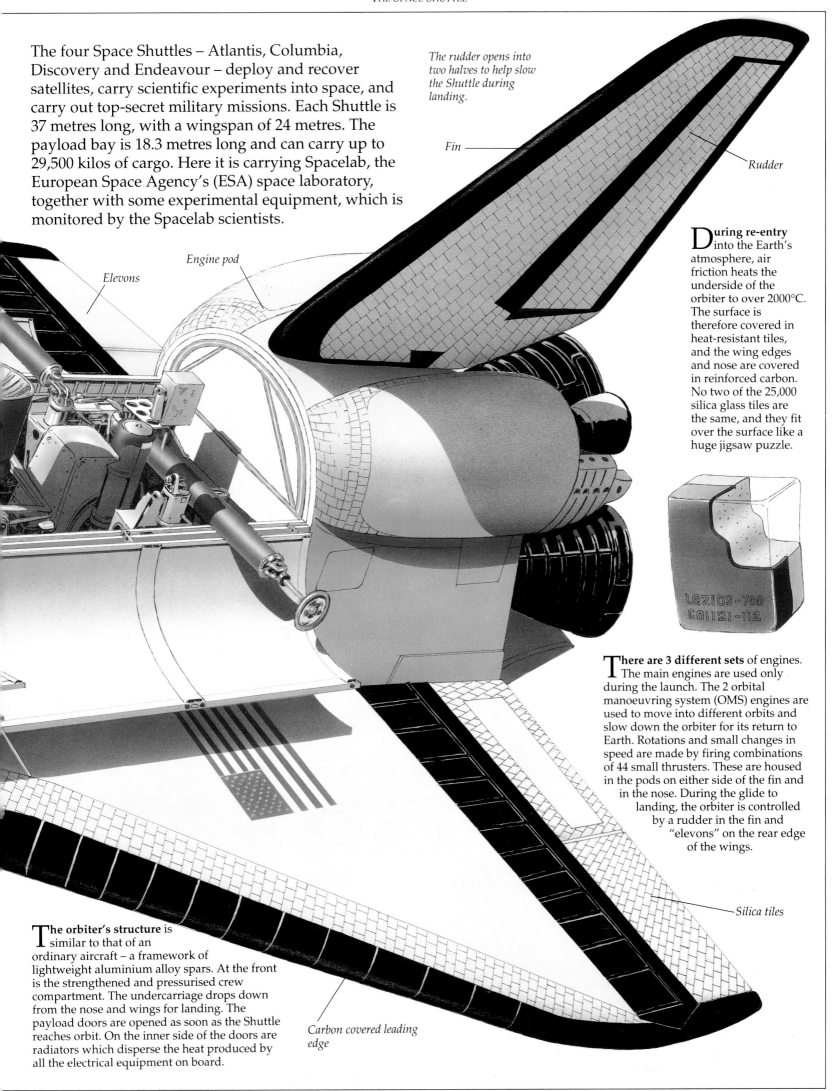

The four Space Shuttles – Atlantis, Columbia, Discovery and Endeavour – deploy and recover satellites, carry scientific experiments into space, and carry out top-secret military missions. Each Shuttle is 37 metres long, with a wingspan of 24 metres. The payload bay is 18.3 metres long and can carry up to 29,500 kilos of cargo. Here it is carrying Spacelab, the European Space Agency's (ESA) space laboratory, together with some experimental equipment, which is monitored by the Spacelab scientists.

The rudder opens into two halves to help slow the Shuttle during landing.

Fin

Rudder

Elevons

Engine pod

During re-entry into the Earth's atmosphere, air friction heats the underside of the orbiter to over 2000°C. The surface is therefore covered in heat-resistant tiles, and the wing edges and nose are covered in reinforced carbon. No two of the 25,000 silica glass tiles are the same, and they fit over the surface like a huge jigsaw puzzle.

LB2103-700
C01121-112

There are 3 different sets of engines. The main engines are used only during the launch. The 2 orbital manoeuvring system (OMS) engines are used to move into different orbits and slow down the orbiter for its return to Earth. Rotations and small changes in speed are made by firing combinations of 44 small thrusters. These are housed in the pods on either side of the fin and in the nose. During the glide to landing, the orbiter is controlled by a rudder in the fin and "elevons" on the rear edge of the wings.

Silica tiles

The orbiter's structure is similar to that of an ordinary aircraft – a framework of lightweight aluminium alloy spars. At the front is the strengthened and pressurised crew compartment. The undercarriage drops down from the nose and wings for landing. The payload doors are opened as soon as the Shuttle reaches orbit. On the inner side of the doors are radiators which disperse the heat produced by all the electrical equipment on board.

Carbon covered leading edge

LAUNCHING THE
Space Shuttle

IT TAKES A MASSIVE PUSH to accelerate the eighty-tonne Space Shuttle orbiter to its "escape velocity" of 40,000 km/h, at which it can evade Earth's gravitational pull. The three main engines in the orbiter have to burn for eight minutes, and for that they need over 1,500,000 litres of liquid hydrogen and liquid oxygen. The orbiter would have to be impractically big to carry that much fuel, so it is launched with a massive fuel tank attached. The tank is jettisoned when the fuel is used up, and is the only part of the Shuttle that cannot be re-used. The full load of fuel weighs 680 tonnes – too much for the orbiter's main engines to lift. So to get the whole thing off the ground and accelerating into space, there are two solid-fuel booster rockets attached to the external fuel tank. Each one contains nearly 500 tonnes of fuel and produces 1,200 tonnes of thrust. Once ignited they burn for two minutes – and they cannot be stopped. At take-off, the combined power of the main engines and booster rockets is equivalent to that produced by 140 jumbo jet engines. A booster fault caused the explosion on board Challenger, the Shuttle lost with its crew in 1986.

The orbiter is attached to the fuel tank and solid-fuel boosters in a massive shed at the Kennedy Space Center at Cape Canaveral. The whole assembly is taken to its launch pad sitting on top of a huge transporter called the Crawler. After the mission, the orbiter lands in California, and returns to Cape Canaveral "piggy back" on a specially adapted Boeing 747.

USA

Crawler transporter

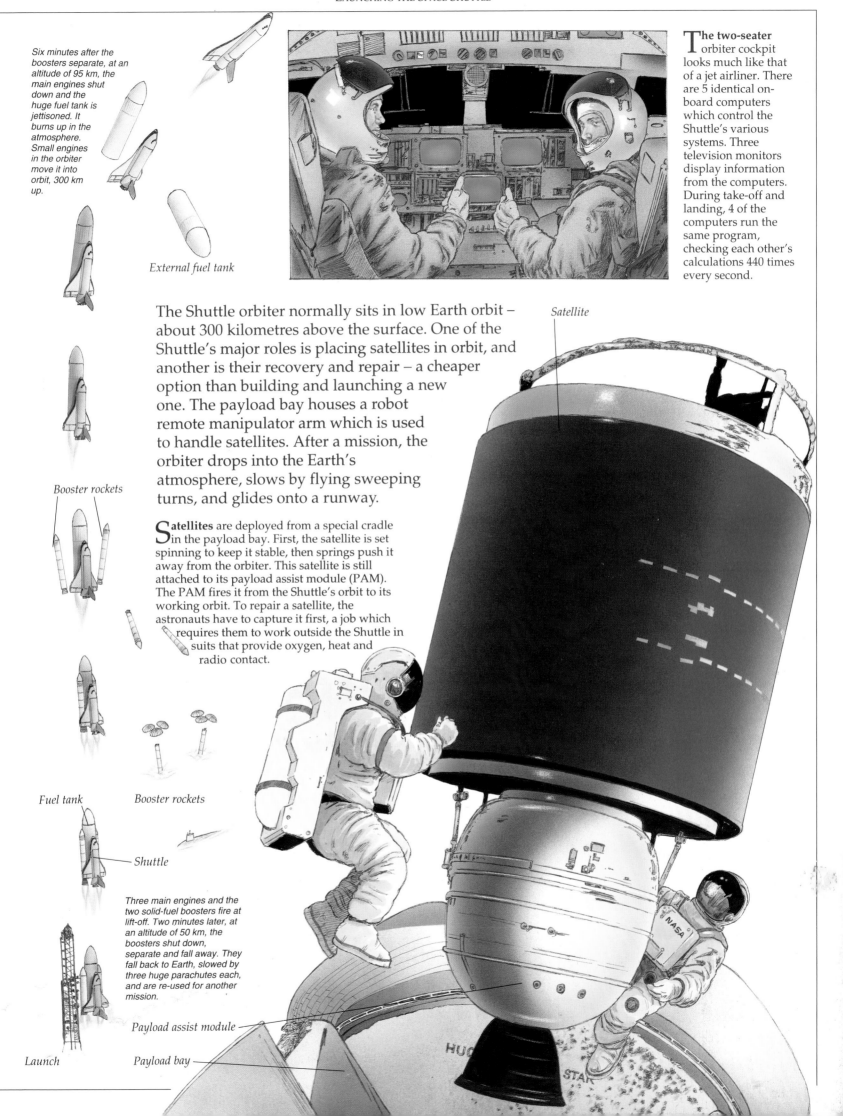

Six minutes after the boosters separate, at an altitude of 95 km, the main engines shut down and the huge fuel tank is jettisoned. It burns up in the atmosphere. Small engines in the orbiter move it into orbit, 300 km up.

External fuel tank

The two-seater orbiter cockpit looks much like that of a jet airliner. There are 5 identical on-board computers which control the Shuttle's various systems. Three television monitors display information from the computers. During take-off and landing, 4 of the computers run the same program, checking each other's calculations 440 times every second.

Satellite

The Shuttle orbiter normally sits in low Earth orbit – about 300 kilometres above the surface. One of the Shuttle's major roles is placing satellites in orbit, and another is their recovery and repair – a cheaper option than building and launching a new one. The payload bay houses a robot remote manipulator arm which is used to handle satellites. After a mission, the orbiter drops into the Earth's atmosphere, slows by flying sweeping turns, and glides onto a runway.

Booster rockets

Satellites are deployed from a special cradle in the payload bay. First, the satellite is set spinning to keep it stable, then springs push it away from the orbiter. This satellite is still attached to its payload assist module (PAM). The PAM fires it from the Shuttle's orbit to its working orbit. To repair a satellite, the astronauts have to capture it first, a job which requires them to work outside the Shuttle in suits that provide oxygen, heat and radio contact.

Fuel tank

Booster rockets

Shuttle

Three main engines and the two solid-fuel boosters fire at lift-off. Two minutes later, at an altitude of 50 km, the boosters shut down, separate and fall away. They fall back to Earth, slowed by three huge parachutes each, and are re-used for another mission.

Launch

Payload assist module

Payload bay

GLOSSARY

Aileron A control surface on the back edge of an aircraft wing, used for side-to-side stability.

Atmospheric pressure The pressure caused by the weight of air in the atmosphere. It decreases with altitude.

Autopilot An electronic system that keeps an aircraft flying automatically at the right height and on the right course.

Avionics The electronic systems of aircraft, used for communications, navigation and aircraft control.

Axle A shaft in a road vehicle or train to which the wheels are attached. Normally, an axle has a wheel at each end.

Ballast Heavy material which is used to increase weight, e.g. for controlling submarines and airships, and for making ships more stable.

Bogie wheels Sets of wheels on locomotives and carriages which can turn to follow the curves of a track.

Boiler The container in which water is boiled to make steam in a steam engine.

Camshaft A shaft on which there are humps. In an engine, as the cam shaft turns, the humps push open the valves.

Cantilever suspension A type of suspension design in motorcycles where the wheel is on the end of a beam which comes out from the chassis.

Clutch A pair of revolving pads which are pushed together or pulled apart to transmit or cut off the power to a vehicle's wheels.

Compressed air Air that is stored in strong tanks at high pressure.

Control surface A part of an aircraft which moves to change the flow of air over the aircraft, and so affects the aircraft's movement.

Cylinder The part of an engine in which expanding steam or ignited fuel pushes the piston up and down, producing movement.

Deploy To place something, such as a satellite, in a pre-arranged position.

Depth charge An underwater bomb used to attack submarines. It explodes, making a shock wave that breaks open the submarine's hull.

Dirigible A balloon or airship whose direction and altitude can be controlled.

Diving bell An air-filled chamber used by divers as a temporary underwater base.

Docking The meeting and attachment in space of two spacecraft, or a spacecraft and space station.

Driving wheels The wheels on a vehicle that are driven round by the engine.

Elevator A control surface on the tailplane of an aircraft used to make the aircraft pitch up or down.

Elevon A control surface used on aircraft with delta (triangular) wings. An elevon is a cross between an aileron and an elevator.

Fin The vertical surface at the back of an aircraft which keeps it going in a straight line. The rudder is mounted on the fin.

Four-stroke A diesel or petrol engine in which there are four stages in each cycle: fuel intake, compression, ignition and exhaust.

Fuselage The tubular section that forms the main body of an aircraft.

Gauge The distance between the two rails on a railway track. Gauges can vary between countries.

Gondola A compartment that hangs underneath an airship, and which may contain the control cabin, accommodation or engines.

Horsepower A unit of power, normally used to measure the power of an engine.

Independent suspension Vehicle suspension where each wheel has its own suspension, rather than in pairs on a suspended axle.

Jettison To abandon something, for example an empty fuel tank.

Kevlar A new type of plastic that is light and very strong.

Life-support system A set of devices on a spacecraft, such as an oxygen supply and heating system, which keeps the crew alive.

Micro-organisms Microscopic living things, such as viruses and bacteria.

Nacelle A pod-like container for an airship engine.

Nuclear reactor A device which produces heat from nuclear reactions. The reactions can be controlled to change the heat given off.

Orbit The path an object follows around a planet. A spacecraft is kept in orbit by its speed and the gravity of the planet.

Periscope An optical device used to see objects that would otherwise be out of sight. For example, a submarine periscope allows the crew to see objects above the water when the submarine is submerged.

Power-to-weight ratio The amount of power an engine produces compared to its weight. A high power-to-weight ratio is best.

Pressurised An aircraft cabin that has air pumped into it so that the passengers can breathe when the aircraft is at high altitude.

Radar A device that detects the position of objects by bouncing radio waves off them.

Radiator A device for getting rid of unwanted heat. For example, in a car, excess heat from the engine is lost from its radiator.

Rolling stock The vehicles that move along the track on a railway, such as locomotives and carriages.

Rudder A control surface on an aircraft or ship which turns from side to side to change its direction.

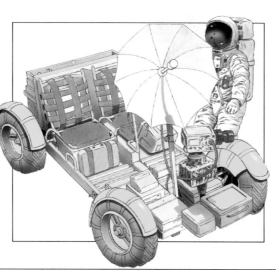

Seismic Concerned with earthquakes, or lunar quakes.

Silencer A part of an engine's exhaust system. It reduces the noise caused by the combustion of the fuel.

Slipway A long, shallow track from a dockyard into the water, down which a ship slides when it is launched.

Sonar A device used to locate underwater objects. It sends out sound waves and detects the echoes that return.

Spark-plug An electrical device which produces a small spark when electricity flows through it. It is used to ignite the petrol and air mixture inside a petrol engine.

Supercharger A pump attached to an internal combustion engine which pumps air into the cylinders. It allows more fuel to be burnt and so increases the engine's power.

Tailplane A small wing at the back of an aircraft which helps to make it stable in flight. The elevators are attached to the tailplane.

Telegraph A simple electrical communication system. Signals are normally transmitted in Morse code – long and short pulses.

Torpedo A long, thin underwater bomb propelled by a small motor.

Turbine A windmill-like device which spins when a gas or liquid passes through it.

Valve A device that opens or closes to control the flow of a gas or liquid. The valves in an internal combustion engine open to let air and fuel in or exhaust gases out.

Weightless The feeling of being in zero gravity, so that you float about. Astronauts in orbit feel weightless.

PRINTED IN BELGIUM BY proost INTERNATIONAL BOOK PRODUCTION